Successful
Diabetic Cookery

Successful Diabetic Cookery

is just one of the books you can buy from the British Diabetic Association. If you would like to know about the others, please write to the BDA, 10, Queen Anne Street, London W1.

Better still, if you are not a member yet, please join us now!

Membership does not cost a lot (see rates below) and in return for your membership fee you will:

● receive six copies of *Balance* a year. That means news of progress in medical care, news about diets and recipes, personalities and practical hints on day-to-day problems.

● have access to a welfare advisory service that will answer your questions on everything from jam-making to life insurance—except of course on individual treatment.

● be able to join any one of over 175 local branches or send your child to a summer camp with other diabetic children.

● play your part in a research programme whose ultimate aim is the defeat of diabetes.

Please remember: the BDA depends entirely upon voluntary support—and that means *your* support.

Free: for one year to children under 16.
50p: for pensioners, widows, students, the unemployed.
£2.50: for Full members.
£5.00: for members living overseas.
£70.00: for life membership. A single payment of £70 may be made or else £10 a year can be paid for seven years under covenant.

Please fill in the membership form.

British Diabetic Association, 10, Queen Anne Street, London W1

– –

To: Secretary-General, British Diabetic Association, 10, Queen Anne Street, London W1.

Please enrol me as a member of the British Diabetic Association, for which I enclose the sum of: £

Use block letters please

Surname ....

First names ....

Address ....

....

Date of birth .... Occupation ....
(*this information will be treated as strictly confidential*)

Date .... Signature...

British Diabetic Association—a company limited by guarantee
Registered office: 10, Queen Anne Street, London W1
Registered in England. Registration No.: 339181

Successful Diabetic Cookery

by
Pamela Robinson
and
Audrey Francis

Pamela Robinson is dietician to the British Diabetic Association.

Acknowledgements

Thanks are due to the following for their help in testing the recipes:

Department ASHE, Cassio College
School of Hotelkeeping, Catering and Tourism, Ealing Technical
    College
Department of Catering, Home and Community Care, Harlow,
    Technical College
Department of Catering, Kilburn Polytechnic
Department of Hotel and Catering Studies, South-East London
    College
Department of Catering, Southgate Technical College
Catering and Domestic Division, Thurrock Technical College
School of Catering and Hotel Administration, Waltham Forest
    College

Cover photography by John Melville
Cover design by Harry Sida
Line drawings by Harry Sida
Editing and production by Prisca Middlemiss BDA
We are grateful to Mrs Iris Kendrick for permission to reprint some recipes from
'Diet Without Tears'
© British Diabetic Association
Printed by F. J. Parsons (Westminster Press Ltd), London and Hastings

Contents

Introduction

Why am I on a diet and what is diabetes?

Let's face it. You enjoy food, and the chances are that you are interested in cooking it. If you were not, you wouldn't be reading this now.

As you read, the words 'diabetic diet' may still be ringing in your ears, suggesting to you a future of lettuce leaves and coleslaw. If so, you are going to be pleasantly surprised: you won't get very far on lettuce and coleslaw as a diabetic! In fact, eating as a diabetic won't be enormously different from eating before.

The only difference is that part of your internal machinery is now out of order. The part we call your insulin factory has broken down.

If you have insulin injections, then your insulin factory has almost stopped production. And the chances are that you are youngish, or you were when your first got diabetes.

If you take tablets or just follow a diet, then your insulin factory has an overtime ban. When your body demands extra insulin the factory refuses to supply it. It is going slow. This may partly be because you are overweight and demanding too much insulin. And it's quite likely, if you are this sort of diabetic, that you were middle-aged or older when you first got diabetes.

What's insulin?

It's like this. When you eat sugary or starchy food (like jam doughnuts) your body must turn the sugar or starch into energy and warmth. First, it breaks down the sugar or starch into simple units, chiefly glucose. The glucose travels round the body in your bloodstream waiting to be called on. Then you have a sudden burst of activity and you want more energy. The glucose is called on by a cell and *together with insulin* it passes into the cell and produces energy.

No insulin, no energy. The glucose cannot pass into the cell without it, and just goes round and round in the blood, collecting in ever larger amounts until it finally spills over into the urine.

So your body is like a car. It's tanked up with fuel (jam doughnuts and other sugary foods) but the battery is flat and so there is no spark to ignite the petrol. The battery, and its spark, is your insulin.

This is where you come in

Your doctor will look after your battery by making sure you have injections or tablets or just lose weight, if you need to.

1

You are in charge of your fuel supply. The sugary foods you eat have to arrive in the right quantities at the right times. That is all a 'diabetic diet' means. The important part of sugary or starchy foods is the *carbohydrate*. There are other parts as well, like fat and vitamins and protein, but these are less important.

All sugary and starchy foods contain carbohydrate. Sugar is pure, 100% carbohydrate and so are boiled sweets. Potatoes are only 20% carbohydrate. Here is a list of the main sources of carbohydrate for you.

Where is carbohydrate found?

Sugar: Sugar itself, glucose, syrup, treacle, jam and marmalade, sweet soft drinks.
Starches: Bread, cereals, flour, and products made with flour, potatoes, rice, maize, pasta.
Milk sugar: All milks, including skimmed milk, contain the carbohydrate called lactose.
Fruit sugar: The carbohydrate fructose is found in all fruits and honey.

Eating as a diabetic

Earlier, we said that eating as a diabetic is not very different from eating normally. Now look at this—a typical day's food:

		Carbohydrate (CHO)
Breakfast:	half a grapefruit	
	eggs and bacon	
	½ slice of toast and marmalade	20
	cup(s) of tea or coffee	
Mid-morning:	coffee and 2 rich tea biscuits	10
Mid-day:	ham salad	
	roll and butter	10
	gooseberry pie	20
	tea or coffee	
Afternoon:	sandwich and tea	10

Evening:	meat loaf	
	carrots and potatoes	20
	ice-cream	10
	tea or coffee	
Bed-time:	cocoa and biscuits	10
Milk in tea or coffee throughout the day		10
(a generous cupful—7 fl oz)		
		120

Swap some of the foods for your own favourite dishes and that is not too different from what you might eat every day, is it? Well, it's a diabetic diet.

The numbers on the right are what make food into a diabetic diet. They tell you how much carbohydrate there is in any one dish. So, starting at the top, there is none in half a grapefruit or in eggs and bacon, but 20 grams of carbohydrate in half a slice of toast and marmalade, 10 grams in coffee and biscuits and so on. Over the whole day, you will have eaten 120 grams of carbohydrate, and *most important,* you will have eaten it gradually over the whole day. (Not all the 120 grams at one fell swoop in an orgy of gluttony—over half a chocolate gâteau, for instance!)

Notes to a diabetic's day's eating

● 120 grams of carbohydrate a day would be about right for a mediumly-active, middle-aged diabetic. If you are a schoolchild, you may eat more than this and will certainly have more at mid-morning and mid-afternoon. If you have a strenuous, energy-consuming job, you may be allowed to eat twice as much carbohydrate as this, perhaps even 250 grams of carbohydrate (CHO) a day.

● No one dish gives you more than 25 grams of carbohydrate (CHO). This lightens the burden of demand on your insulin factory at any one time. Remember: aim to spread your carbohydrate gradually throughout the day.

● This is a must. Diabetics just cannot miss breakfast. And eggs and bacon are not enough; you must have cereal or toast as well, something with carbohydrate (CHO) in.

● Don't worry, we are not condemning you to a life-time of ham salads for lunch and meat pies in the evening. You would be bored to distraction—and disobedience, too, no doubt! What you have to bear in mind is the *total carbohydrate* for each meal. For lunch on our day's

3

eating, it is 30 grams of carbohydrate (CHO). We have allowed 20 for gooseberry pie and 10 for a roll. Suppose you loath gooseberry pie? Then use your 20 grams on blackberry and apple crumble (recipe, see page 127) or on lime trifle (recipe, see page 135), or whatever takes your fancy and gives you the right amount of carbohydrate (CHO).

Suppose you abhor puddings. Then you have 30 grams for your meat course. You could have pizza (recipe, see page 80) or steak and kidney hotpot (recipe, see page 60) as well as a helping of potato or chips. Your doctor will tell you how much carbohydrate you can have. You ring the changes. Swap and exchange to your palate's delight.

Use any of the recipes in this book. Just check the carbohydrate (CHO) figure at the top of the recipe and count it in to your meal.

Swap and exchange

This system of swapping is called using *exchanges*. One exchange contains 10 grams of carbohydrate and you can swap it for any other. One apple has 10 grams of carbohydrate (CHO) and so has an orange. Have one or the other at mid-morning instead of biscuits (not both!). To help you with exchanges there is a list of them on pages 183 to 187.

What do I do when I am hungry?

The answer to this one is much easier for diabetics than for slimmers. Because while virtually all foods contain calories (which slimmers have to watch) quite a few foods contain no carbohydrate (which diabetics have to watch). We call them free foods, and you can eat them at will when you are hungry. Have a look on pages 188 to 189, where there is quite a list of free foods for you to indulge in. There are even some carbohydrate-free recipes, like sausage and liver pâté on page 54, or coffee whip on page 128.

Protein and fat

We have talked a lot about carbohydrate (CHO) because it is specially important to diabetics. But it is also important to eat a well-balanced mixture of foods, including proteins and fats.

Proteins keep your body in good repair and help children to grow—which is why children need more protein than older people. You will find protein in meat, cheese, fish, eggs and milk; there's a lot of it in soya products, peas, beans and lentils as well.

Fats are useful because they give you energy and keep you warm in winter. They also supply the important vitamins A, D, E and K. Apart from obvious places like butter, margarine and cooking oil, fat is found in cheese, cream, oily fish and in meat. Watch these foods if you are overweight, though; one ounce of butter gives you 252 calories—more than you should have at one meal!

Losing weight?

You aren't alone: there are perhaps nearly half a million other overweight diabetics in Britain today. They manage to lose weight, and so can you, if you try. If you do not want to lose weight, you will not. It is up to you!

Being fat (obesity, as doctors call it) has one main cause: eating too much. 'Too much' varies enormously from person to person, but if you are overweight, you have been eating more than your body needs. Too much food means too many calories means fat.

To lose weight, you have to eat less food. It is not, after all, so much what you eat as how much. Being fat may have been a sign of wealth in the Middle Ages, but no longer! Overweight burdens down your heart, raises your life insurance premiums, shortens your life and makes your diabetes worse. So you are better off thinner.

To lose weight you must cut back your calorie intake to 1000 calories or so a day. What you will eat will look something like this:

Breakfast:	half a grapefruit
	one egg (not fried)
	one small slice of toast with a very little butter or a little more Outline
	tea or coffee with milk
Mid-morning:	tea or coffee with milk
Mid-day:	a small helping (2 oz (55 g)) of meat *or* 4 oz (115 g) fish *or* 1–2 eggs
	green vegetables or salad
	a small helping (2 oz (55 g)) potato
	fruit (1 piece)
Tea:	a hot drink—tea, coffee, Bovril or Marmite
Evening:	as lunch
Bed-time:	hot drink and fruit

Milk in tea or coffee throughout the day: 7 fl oz (200 ml).

This is not half so plain as it looks: if you use a good variety of interesting vegetables and fruit you can make yourself an exciting slimming menu, though this is easier said than done in winter!

Notes to the slimmer's day's eating

- No one meal should contain more than 250 Calories.
- Virtually all foods contain calories.
- Don't fry your food: grill it, roast it, braise it or boil it instead.
- Watch out for nibbling to make up for the carbohydrate you are missing. Cheese is particularly dangerous as it is tempting and carbohydrate-free, but 1 oz gives 120 Calories.
- Skimmed milk is useful. So is Outline (margarine mixed with water). Ryvita and other crispbreads can also help, but *only* if you stick to the rest of your diet!
- Diabetic products do not help. They are usually sweetened with sorbitol or fructose, which have just as many calories as sugar. Forget them, except for the fruit squashes and salad dressing (not salad cream) which are alright. And the low-calorie drinks are fine. So are Bovril and Marmite.
- If you have to lose weight, the best thing is to get on with it and not cheat. If you cheat on your diet, you are prolonging the agony and it is your agony, not your doctor's, dietician's, wife's or husband's.

How to avoid sugar: artificial sweeteners

Saccharin. Of the wide variety of sugar-substitutes on the market, the best for all diabetics is saccharin. This is because it provides neither carbohydrate nor calories and so weight-watching diabetics can use it freely. Brand names for saccharin include Saxin, Sweetex and Hermesetas.

Saccharin-mixes. Keep well away from sweeteners which consist of saccharin mixed with sugar. They are not suitable for diabetics, even if the amount of sugar in the mix does seem small. Brand names of this type of sweetener are Sucron and Sugarlite.

Sorbitol. This is a common sweetener for diabetics, which contains no carbohydrate but just as many calories as sugar—112 Calories per ounce. It will not do for you if you are overweight, but for other diabetics it is especially useful in cooking, giving bulk which saccharin lacks. Sorbitol is only about half as sweet as sugar and has the disadvantage that it can cause diarrhoea if eaten in more than small quantities. The BDA recommends that you take no more than 2 oz (55 g) a day and that you spread your intake evenly over the day.

Fructose. Fructose, or fruit sugar, is a carbohydrate but most of it does not need insulin to turn it into energy for your body's needs. As it has as many calories as sugar, it is not suitable for the overweight, but it has the advantage of being twice as sweet as sugar, so you only need use half as much. Like Sorbitol, only 2 oz (55 g) a day should be taken and neither should *ever* be used neat—sprinkled on fruit or in hot drinks, for example.

Oven temperatures

Fahrenheit °F	Celsius °C	Gas Mark
150	70	
175	80	
200	100	
225	110	$\frac{1}{4}$
250	120	$\frac{1}{2}$
275	140	1
300	150	2
325	160	3
350	180	4
375	190	5
400	200	6
425	220	7
450	230	8
475	240	9
500	260	
525	270	
550	290	

Cooking hints

Acid Fruit. A pinch of bicarbonate of soda added during cooking will make the fruit taste less sour and enhance the effect of any sweetener used.

Artificial Sweeteners. See page 6.

Baking Blind. Preheat the oven to 400°F/Mark 6.

Line a flan tin or pie plate with shortcrust pastry, prick the base and bake for 10 minutes before putting in the filling.

Alternatively, after lining the tin with pastry, cover the base with greaseproof paper or foil, spread with a handful of dried beans and bake for 15 minutes.

Remove the foil or paper and beans before filling.

Eggs. When eggs are to be separated and the whites beaten until stiff, it is advisable to use eggs which are at least 4 days old. New-laid eggs do not beat well.

In some recipes, only the whites or yolks are used. Here are some suggestions for using left-overs.

Whites, beaten until stiff, can be used in:
Dessert decorations: fold into whipped cream to lighten the texture and reduce the calorie value
Fluffy omelettes
Fruit purées
Jellies: fold in as the jelly is beginning to set. This gives a fluffy texture
Meringues
Soufflés
Topping shepherd's pie or fish pie: fold into the mashed potato to lighten it and increase its bulk

Yolks can be used in:
Dipping fish, etc., before breadcrumbing and frying
Mashed potato: beat in just before serving
Mayonnaise
Omelettes: an extra yolk, added to 2 or 3 eggs, improves the texture
Pastry: paint on just before a pie is put in the oven to give the pastry a glaze
Salads: a yolk placed in a cup and steamed while other food is cooking will set and can then be chopped finely and used to decorate salads

Scrambled eggs: a yolk added to 2 or 3 eggs makes a nice, rich-looking dish.

Gelatine.   Sprinkle the crystals on a little cold water or other cold liquid in a cup and leave to soften for 5 minutes. Then place the cup in a pan of hot (not boiling) water and stir until completely dissolved.

1 level teaspoon of gelatine will set an average teacup of liquid.

3 level teaspoons ($\frac{1}{2}$ oz (15 g)) will set 1 pint (570 ml).

In very hot weather, if a refrigerator is not available for setting, a little extra gelatine may be necessary.

Pastry.   See Basic Recipes, pages 14 to 15.

Purées.   To reduce fruits or vegetables to a purée, cook until soft and then rub through a sieve. Alternatively, they can be put through a food mill or electric liquidiser.

Roux.   This is the basis of many sauces. To make it, melt fat over a low heat and sift in flour. Return the pan to the heat and stir until a 'roux' forms which will leave the sides of the pan clean. Do not allow it to brown unless you want a brown sauce.

Add cold liquid gradually, stirring all the time. If lumps start to form, withdraw the pan from the heat and beat vigorously before adding any more liquid.

Saccharin.   Do not add saccharin to fruit before cooking or you will get a bitter, metallic taste. Crush the tablets, dissolve them in a little warm water and add them after the fruit has been removed from the heat. Saccharin may be added to milk puddings before cooking.

According to the number of tablets you take in a cup of tea or coffee, the same number per serving when cooking will probably suit your palate.

Sorbitol.   When you are using sorbitol in making cakes or puddings, remember that it needs much more beating than sugar—at least 5 minutes. Sorbitol syrup can be made by adding 3 parts of water to 7 parts of sorbitol.

Soufflés.   To prepare a soufflé dish, grease it well and then wrap foil or greaseproof paper round the outside to project about 2 in above the rim. Secure this with string or sellotape. Remove before serving.

Tomatoes.   Tomatoes (and peaches) can be peeled easily if a few slits are made in the skin and the fruits then immersed first in boiling water for 2 minutes and then plunged into cold water.

Yeast.   See Introduction to Bakery Section, page 146.

Adapting your own recipes

Once you have got used to your diabetes and your new diet you may well find yourself hankering after a favourite old recipe from the days before diabetes. This chapter is written to show you that you can use your old favourites so long as you count the carbohydrate—we'll show you how—and how to adapt them to fit in with your new diet.

First you will need an exchange list which you will find on pages 183 to 187. Once you have this, you can check the amount of carbohydrate in the ingredients in your recipe. Then all you need do is to add up the total carbohydrate in the recipe and divide by the number of portions.

Let's suppose the thought of a chicken casserole is irresistible. These are the ingredients on your time-tested recipe for four people:

a chicken—weighing about 2¼ lb
1 medium onion, 1 stick celery
2 oz mushrooms
1 stock cube
½ pint water
½ oz flour
salt and pepper to taste

Chicken, as every well-educated diabetic knows, has no carbohydrate. Nor do most stock cubes, water of course or salt and pepper. And vegetables only contain small amounts of carbohydrate and in this recipe they are not worth counting in. Which only leaves the flour.

The exchange list will tell you that one level tablespoon of flour weighs ½ oz (15 g) and gives 10 g of carbohydrate. So this recipe contains a total of 10 g of carbohydrate. As it is for four people, you can divide the 10 g by 4, which leaves you with only 2½ grams. Hardly worth counting at all.

Now let's suppose it is a chicken pie you are secretly longing for. Your recipe is for four people again and has these ingredients:

Pastry:
6 oz flour   1½ oz margarine
1½ oz cooking fat   1 fl oz water

Filling:
1 chicken   teaspoon dried herbs
1 medium onion   ½–¾ pint stock
2 oz mushrooms   ½ oz flour
tablespoon parsley

The only carbohydrate in the filling is in the flour and as in the chicken casserole it gives 10 g of carbohydrate. Parsley and herbs are carbohydrate-free.

That leaves the pastry. Cooking fat and margarine have no carbohydrate, but flour naturally does. It has 20 g of carbohydrate per ounce, which means that 6 oz will give you 120 g of carbohydrate.

Now you can add the 120 g in the pastry to the 10 g in the filling. 130 g of carbohydrate for the whole pie. The pie is for four people, so divide 130 by 4 for your portion of carbohydrate: $32\frac{1}{2}$ g. Quite high, but alright for people with a meal allowance of 40 g or more.

You may now decide it is too high for you, but you still need not abandon the idea of that mouth-watering pie. Why not alter the recipe to give less carbohydrate? You could cut down on the flour in the pastry by using 4 oz instead of 6 oz. It will give you a thinner pastry, but much less carbohydrate. 4 oz of flour will give you only 80 g of carbohydrate, plus the 10 g from the filling, to total 90 g. Divide by the four portions and you have $22\frac{1}{2}$ g of carbohydrate. That's better.

Twenty-two and a half is an awkward figure. If you are not sure whether to round it up to 25 or down to 20, it is better to round it up.

Why, you may well ask, must you round it up? To allow for the vegetables, all of which contain small amounts of carbohydrate, too small to bother calculating but worth allowing for by rounding up.

Cake recipes, however tempting, pose a greater problem, partly because nearly everything in the cake needs to be counted into the total carbohydrate. To help you count, here is a list of normal cake ingredients. The figures on the right show the amount of carbohydrate per ounce.

	grams CHO per oz		grams CHO per oz
Almonds	$1\frac{1}{2}$	Honey	21
Angelica	22	Mixed fruit	18
Black treacle	19	Mixed peel	17
Cocoa	10	Raisins	18
Currants	18	Sugar, all types	28
Dates	18	Sultanas	18
Desiccated coconut	1	Syrup	22
Flour	20	Walnuts	$1\frac{1}{2}$
Glacé cherries	15		

Let's suppose you had the following recipe for a fruit cake cutting into 12 slices.

6 oz self-raising flour	5 fl oz milk
4 oz margarine	dessertspoon of vinegar
$4\frac{1}{2}$ oz sugar	teaspoon of bicarbonate of soda
6 oz mixed fruit	5 or 6 drops lemon or orange essence

11

The amount of carbohydrate in the ingredients would be as follows:

	grams CHO
6 oz self-raising flour	120
4 oz margarine	0
4½ oz sugar	126
6 oz mixed fruit	108
5 fl oz milk	7
dessertspoon of vinegar	0
teaspoon of bicarbonate of soda	0
5 drops of lemon essence	0
	361

So divide the total CHO by the number of slices — 361 divided by 12 equals 30 grams CHO per slice.

This is quite high but the recipe can be adapted. First of all, the sugar can go: it can be replaced by sorbitol. Thus the total CHO (361) less the CHO from the sugar (126) gives a new total of 235. Divide this by 12 and it gives you almost exactly 20 grams CHO per slice.

You can reduce the CHO still further by cutting down the amount of dried fruit from 6 oz to 3½ oz. Your recipe would now look like this:

	grams CHO
6 oz self-raising flour	120
4 oz margarine	0
4½ oz sorbitol	0
3½ oz mixed fruit	63
5 fl oz milk	7
dessertspoon of vinegar	0
teaspoon bicarbonate of soda	0
5 drops lemon essence	0
	190

190 divided by 12 equals 15 grams CHO per slice. Just half the original figure.

Substituting sorbitol for sugar does not always work; sometimes it is necessary to use half sugar and half sorbitol. This has been done in the Chocolate Cake recipe on page 154.

It is impossible to make a light sponge cake with sorbitol, but by using another artificial sweetener, fructose, with sugar a reasonable result can be achieved. See the Coffee Sponge recipe on page 156.

Basic recipes

Shortcrust pastry

4 servings   *Each serving 20 CHO   222 Cals*

4 oz plain flour   115 g plain flour
1 oz margarine   30 g margarine
1 oz lard   30 g lard
½ teaspoon salt   ½ teaspoon salt
cold water   cold water

Sift the flour and salt into a mixing bowl, cut the fat into small pieces
and drop into the flour.

Rub between the finger-tips and thumbs until the fat and flour take on
the consistency of fine breadcrumbs. This should be done as
quickly and lightly as possible.

Add water gradually, mixing with the blade of a knife, until the dough
is just moist enough to cling together. Then, with lightly-floured
hands, roll it into a ball.

Leave in a cool place for half an hour before rolling the pastry out, on a
floured board, to the required shape.

Flaky pastry

8 servings   *Each serving 20 CHO   269 Cals*

8 oz plain flour	225 g plain flour
6 oz butter or margarine	170 g butter or margarine
1 level teaspoon salt	1 level teaspoon salt
cold water	cold water

Sift the flour and salt into a mixing bowl.

Divide the fat into four, cut one quarter into small pieces and rub this into the flour.

Add the water gradually, mixing with a knife blade, until an elastic dough is formed that can be rolled into a ball.

Roll out on a lightly-floured board to an oblong shape.

Cut another quarter of the fat into pieces, dot the centre two-thirds of the pastry and fold into an envelope by turning over the unfatted third.

Rest the pastry in a cool place for at least 15 minutes before rolling it again into an oblong. Dot with fat, fold and chill.

Repeat the process until all the fat is used.

French dressing

Each 25 ml (1 fl oz) serving   *Negligible CHO   180 Cals*

4 fl oz olive or other vegetable
  oil
2 fl oz wine vinegar
½ teaspoon castor sugar
¼ teaspoon French mustard
salt or garlic salt
black pepper

115 ml olive or other vegetable
  oil
55 ml wine vinegar
½ teaspoon castor sugar
½ teaspoon French mustard
salt or garlic salt
black pepper

Beat all the ingredients together and put in a covered jar.
Shake well before use.
If stored in a cool place, the dressing can be kept for several days.

Mayonnaise

4 servings   *Each serving nil CHO   275 Cals*

4 fl oz olive oil
1 egg yolk
1 teaspoon wine vinegar
seasoning

115 ml olive oil
1 egg yolk
1 teaspoon wine vinegar
seasoning

Put the egg yolk, seasoning and a few drops of vinegar into a bowl and
  beat in the oil a drop at a time until the mixture becomes thick and
  creamy. It is important to add the oil gradually at this stage or the
  mayonnaise will not thicken.
The rest of the oil can then be beaten in a teaspoon at a time.
Add the remaining vinegar and continue beating until the mixture is
  thick and smooth.

16

Gravy

4 servings   *Each serving negligible CHO*
                                47 Cals

½ oz gravy mix   15 g gravy mix
½ pint water   285 ml water
1 stock cube   1 stock cube
cooking juices from meat or   cooking juices from meat or
    poultry   poultry

Blend the gravy mix with a little of the water.

After removing the meat from the roasting pan, pour off any excess fat
    leaving all the meat juices behind.

Add the remaining water to the roasting tin, crumble in the stock cube
    and bring to the boil.

Withdraw from the heat, add the gravy mix and return to the boil,
    stirring all the time.

White sauce (with stock)

½ pint (285 ml) of sauce   *20 CHO   325 Cals*

1 oz flour	30 g flour
1 oz butter or margarine	30 g butter or margarine
½ pint chicken stock	285 ml chicken stock
seasoning	seasoning

Melt the fat over a low heat, remove the pan from the heat and sift in the flour.

Return the pan to the heat and stir until a roux is formed that will leave the sides of the pan. Do not allow to brown.

Add the stock gradually, stirring all the time. If lumps start to form, withdraw the pan from the heat and beat the sauce vigorously before adding more liquid.

Check the seasoning before use.

Béchamel (white sauce with milk)

½ pint (285 ml) of sauce   *35 CHO   520 Cals*

1 oz flour	30 g flour
1 oz butter or margarine	30 g butter or margarine
½ pint milk	285 ml milk
1 small onion	1 small onion
6 cloves	6 cloves
1 bay leaf, optional	1 bay leaf, optional
salt and pepper	salt and pepper

Spike the peeled onion with cloves and put it in a saucepan with the
milk, salt and bay leaf. Bring to the boil and simmer very gently
for about 15 minutes.

Strain the milk into a jug and clean the pan.

Melt the fat over a low heat, remove the pan from the heat and sift in
the flour.

Return the pan to the heat and stir until a roux is formed that will leave
the sides of the pan. Do not allow to brown.

Add the flavoured milk, stirring all the time. If lumps start to form,
withdraw the pan from the heat and beat the sauce vigorously
before adding more liquid.

Check the seasoning before use.

Cheese sauce

½ *pint sauce*   *35 CHO   1000 Cals*

½ pint béchamel sauce   285 ml béchamel sauce
  (see p. 19)   (see p. 19)
4 oz grated cheese   115 g grated cheese

Add the grated cheese to the béchamel sauce and stir over a low heat
until melted.

Egg sauce

½ *pint sauce*   *35 CHO   704 Cals*

½ pint béchamel sauce   285 ml béchamel sauce
  (see p. 19)   (see p. 19)
2 hard-boiled eggs   2 hard-boiled eggs

Chop the hard-boiled eggs finely and add to the béchamel sauce. Warm
the sauce through.

Parsley sauce

½ *pint sauce*   *35 CHO   520 Cals*

½ pint béchamel sauce   285 ml béchamel sauce
  (see p. 19)   (see p. 19)
2 tablespoons chopped parsley   2 tablespoons chopped parsley

Mix the chopped parsley into the béchamel sauce. Heat through.

Tomato sauce

$\frac{3}{4}$ *pint (425 ml)*	*30 CHO 411 Cals*

1 lb fresh tomatoes	455 g fresh tomatoes
or	or
15 oz tin tomatoes	425 g tin tomatoes
1 oz flour	30 g flour
1 oz butter or margarine	30 g butter or margarine
$\frac{1}{2}$ pint stock	285 ml stock
2 teaspoons tomato purée, optional	2 teaspoons tomato purée, optional
1 teaspoon dried mixed herbs	1 teaspoon dried mixed herbs
seasoning	seasoning

If fresh tomatoes are used, remove the skins.

Make a sauce with the flour, butter and stock. (See p. 9.)

Add the tomatoes, herbs, tomato purée and seasoning, cover the pan, bring to the boil and cook very gently for about 25 minutes. Stir from time to time.

Rub the mixture through a sieve, return to the pan and reheat the sauce before use.

Brown stock

3¼ lb shin of beef bones	1½ kg shin of beef bones
5¼ pints vegetable water	3 litres vegetable water
or	or
water	water
1 large onion	1 large onion
2 large carrots	2 large carrots
1 small turnip	1 small turnip
2 celery sticks	2 celery sticks
1 bouquet garni	1 bouquet garni
or	or
1 heaped teaspoon mixed dried herbs	1 heaped teaspoon mixed dried herbs
6 peppercorns	6 peppercorns
salt	salt

Crack the bones (or ask your butcher to do this) and place them in a large saucepan.

Trim and chop the root vegetables roughly and add to the pan with the herbs and water.

Bring to the boil, skim off the scum, cover the pan and simmer gently for about 3 hours. Skim again at intervals to remove any further scum.

Strain and leave in a cool place.

When quite cold, remove the layer of fat which will have formed.

Fortified with a little Bovril or Marmite, this stock makes a good clear soup.

NOTE: *When recipes indicate brown stock, a beef bouillon cube can be used instead but this will not have as much flavour as a bone-based stock.*

Chicken stock

Each serving negligible CHO

1 chicken carcase (or the equivalent amount of turkey or game bones)

5¼ pints water

1 onion

2 carrots

1 small turnip, optional

2 celery sticks, optional

1 bouquet garni
   or
1 level teaspoon mixed dried herbs

4 peppercorns

salt

1 chicken carcase (or the equivalent amount of turkey or game bones)

3 litres water

1 onion

2 carrots

1 small turnip, optional

2 celery sticks, optional

1 bouquet garni
   or
1 level teaspoon mixed dried herbs

4 peppercorns

salt

Prepare the vegetables and put with the other ingredients in a large saucepan.

Bring to the boil and simmer gently for about 2 hours. If a pressure cooker is used the time will be reduced to about 20 minutes.

Strain and cool. Store in a refrigerator until required.

NOTE: *Where recipes indicate chicken stock, a chicken bouillon cube may be used instead but the flavour will not be so good.*

Sage & onion stuffing

4 servings   *Each serving 10 CHO   134 Cals*

3 oz breadcrumbs	85 g breadcrumbs
1 small onion	1 small onion
1 small egg	1 small egg
1 oz dripping or butter	30 g dripping or butter
1 teaspoon dried sage	1 teaspoon dried sage
or	or
6 sage leaves, chopped	6 sage leaves, chopped
salt and pepper	salt and pepper

Preheat the oven to 350°F/Mark 4.

Peel and chop the onion finely and fry it in heated dripping until soft.

Combine the onion with all the other ingredients and bind with the egg. Season to taste.

Form into 4 balls and bake round the meat or poultry for the final 20 minutes of cooking.

Sausage forcemeat

4 servings   *Each serving 5 CHO   84 Cals*

$\frac{2}{3}$ oz breadcrumbs	20 g breadcrumbs
3 oz sausage meat (2 large sausages, skinned)	85 g sausage meat (2 large sausages, skinned)
$\frac{1}{2}$ teaspoon dried herbs	$\frac{1}{2}$ teaspoon dried herbs
grated rind of half a lemon, optional	grated rind of half a lemon, optional
2 teaspoons stock	2 teaspoons stock

Mix all the ingredients together well and use for stuffing game or poultry.

If preferred, the forcemeat can be formed into 4 sausages and placed round the bird in the baking tin for the final 25 minutes of cooking.

24

Yorkshire pudding

8 puddings   *Each pudding 5 CHO   74 Cals*

2 oz flour	55 g flour
1 egg	1 egg
2 fl oz milk	55 ml milk
3 fl oz water	85 ml water
salt	salt
1 oz cooking fat	30 g cooking fat

Preheat the oven to 450°F/Mark 8.

Mix the flour with a pinch of salt.

Beat together the egg, milk and water. Add gradually to the flour, beating all the time until the batter is smooth. Leave to stand for 1 hour.

Divide the cooking fat between 8 patty pans and heat in the oven until the fat is very hot.

Pour in the batter and bake for 15 minutes.

Soups

A clear soup can be taken as a carbohydrate and Calorie free 'extra'. It is therefore a good filler when you are hungry and is warming on a cold day.

Bones and vegetables make good stock, either for a clear soup or as the base for a thick soup. so do not throw them away!

Some of the recipes, like the lentil and bacon soup, are a meal in themselves and can be reheated to give several light midday meals or suppers. When reheating soups or stews, be sure to bring them to the boil and cook for several minutes as a precaution against food poisoning.

In times of illness, soup can be a good way of taking your carbohydrate allowance when sweet drinks do not tempt the appetite.

Chicken soup

4 servings   *Each serving 5 CHO   125 Cals*

1½ pints chicken stock	850 ml chicken stock
½ oz butter or margarine	15 g butter or margarine
½ oz flour	15 g flour
4 fl oz single cream	115 ml single cream
chopped parsley or chives	chopped parsley or chives
seasoning	seasoning

Make a roux with the flour and the butter, add the stock and stir until smooth and beginning to boil. Lower the heat and simmer very gently for about 30 minutes.

Check the seasoning and just before serving add the cream and sprinkle with parsley or chives.

Chicken soup (Summer)

2 servings   *Each serving 10 CHO   200 Cals*

1 small tin of condensed cream of chicken soup	1 small tin of condensed cream of chicken soup
1 level teaspoon of curry powder	1 level teaspoon of curry powder
4 fl oz milk	115 ml milk
1 teaspoon of fresh lemon juice	1 teaspoon of fresh lemon juice
2 fl oz single cream	55 ml single cream
chopped parsley or chives	chopped parsley or chives

Sieve the soup, milk and curry powder. To ensure that the curry powder blends in, it may be mixed with a little water before adding to the soup.

Leave to chill and, just before serving, stir in the lemon juice and cream and add an ice cube to each dish.

Garnish with chopped parsley.

Cream of celery soup

4 servings   *Each serving 5 CHO   97 Cals*

12 oz celery sticks, trimmed   340 g celery sticks, trimmed
2 oz potatoes, peeled   55 g potatoes, peeled
2 medium leeks (white part only)   2 medium leeks (white part only)
1 medium onion   1 medium onion
1 oz butter or margarine   30 g butter or margarine
7 fl oz milk   200 ml milk
$\frac{3}{4}$ pint chicken stock   425 ml chicken stock
2 tablespoons of cream   2 tablespoons of cream
celery salt, optional   celery salt, optional
salt and pepper   salt and pepper

Clean and chop all the vegetables and fry them gently in the heated
    butter in a large heavy saucepan for a few minutes, stirring until
    all are coated with butter. Cover the pan and continue cooking
    over a very low heat for about 15 minutes, shaking the pan from
    time to time to prevent sticking.
Pour on the stock and milk, add seasoning, bring to the boil and
    simmer gently until all the vegetables are soft (about 25 minutes).
Allow to cool and reduce to a purée.
Just before serving add the cream.

French onion soup

4 servings   *Each serving 5 CHO   180 Cals*

1¾ pints chicken stock	1 litre chicken stock
1 lb onions	455 g onions
1 oz butter or margarine	30 g butter or margarine
1 fl oz cooking oil	30 ml cooking oil
2 teaspoons tomato purée	2 teaspoons tomato purée
2 teaspoons of grated Cheddar cheese	2 teaspoons of grated Cheddar cheese
seasoning	seasoning

Peel and slice the onions thinly.

Heat the butter and the oil together in a large saucepan over a low heat.

Add the onions and cook without a lid until they are golden brown.
Stir from time to time and do not let the onions get crisp.

Add the stock, seasoning and tomato purée. Check the flavour.* Bring
to the boil and simmer for about 45 minutes.

Serve very hot and sprinkled, if liked, with grated cheese.

* *To give the soup a stronger flavour, one or two stock cubes can be
added at this stage.*

Leek and potato soup

4 servings   *Each serving 5 CHO   125 Cals*

4 oz potatoes   115 g potatoes
2 large or 4 small leeks   2 large or 4 small leeks
1 oz butter or margarine   30 g butter or margarine
1 pint chicken stock   570 ml chicken stock
2 fl oz single cream   55 ml single cream
chopped parsley or chives   chopped parsley or chives
seasoning   seasoning

Peel and dice the potatoes. Clean the leeks well, cut down the centre
and chop into short strips.
Melt the butter and fry the potatoes and leeks gently in a saucepan for
a few minutes.
Add the stock and the seasoning, cover the pan and simmer for about
20 minutes until the vegetables are soft.
Just before serving add the cream and garnish with parsley or chives.
NOTE: *This soup may be served chilled.*

Lentil and bacon soup

6 servings   *Each serving 15 CHO   207 Cals*

6 oz lentils	170 g lentils
1 small bacon knuckle	1 small bacon knuckle
½ oz dripping (preferably pork)	15 g dripping (preferably pork)
1 large or 2 small onions	1 large or 2 small onions
1½–2 pints water	1 litre water
seasoning	seasoning

Soak the lentils overnight in twice as much water as is necessary to cover them.

In the morning fry the bacon to seal it.

Strain the lentils and make the water up to 1½ pints and put into a pan with the bacon.

Bring to the boil and simmer in a covered pan for 1½ hours, or pressure cook for 20 minutes.

Withdraw from the heat and remove the bacon knuckle, cool the lentil mixture and purée it.

Melt the dripping in a large saucepan and fry the chopped onion until soft but not brown; add this to the soup.

Remove the rind from the bacon, cut the meat from the bone, chop it and add it to the soup.

Check the seasoning, re-heat and serve.

NOTE: *This is suitable for a main course.*

31

Minestrone

4 servings   *Each serving 5 CHO   187 Cals*

1 medium onion	1 medium onion
8 oz carrots	225 g carrots
8 oz globe artichokes, optional	225 g globe artichokes, optional
small piece of turnip	small piece of turnip
2 celery sticks	2 celery sticks
1 fl oz cooking oil	30 ml cooking oil
$1\frac{3}{4}$ pints stock	1 litre stock
1 teaspoon mixed herbs	1 teaspoon mixed herbs
2 teaspoons of tomato purée	2 teaspoons of tomato purée
$\frac{1}{2}$ oz of spaghetti	15 g spaghetti
2 oz grated cheese	55 g grated cheese
chopped parsley	chopped parsley
seasoning	seasoning

Trim the vegetables and chop them finely.

Melt the oil in a large saucepan and fry the vegetables for a few minutes, but do not let them brown.

Add the stock, herbs and seasoning, bring to the boil, cover the pan and simmer for about 15 minutes.

Break the spaghetti into small pieces and add it with the tomato purée to the soup.

Cover the pan and simmer for a further 15 minutes or until the vegetables and the spaghetti are soft.

Sprinkle with parsley and serve with grated cheese.

Mushroom soup

2 servings   *Each serving 10 CHO   160 Cals*

4 oz button mushrooms	115 g button mushrooms
1 small onion	1 small onion
½ oz butter or margarine	15 g butter or margarine
½ oz flour	15 g flour
8 fl oz chicken stock	225 ml chicken stock
5 fl oz milk	140 ml milk
seasoning	seasoning

Wash the mushrooms and chop them finely.

Peel and slice the onion.

Heat the butter in a saucepan and cook the onion gently until soft; then add the mushrooms to the pan and cook for a further 5 minutes.

Blend in the flour, add the stock and stir until the soup thickens.

Add the milk and simmer very slowly for about 10 minutes.

Cool and reduce to a purée (see p. 9).

Check the seasoning and re-heat before serving.

Pea soup

$\frac{1}{2}$ lb split peas	225 g split peas
2 onions	2 onions
1 carrot	1 carrot
2 oz fat	55 g fat
2 pints stock or water	1125 ml stock or water
2 tablespoons top-of-the-milk	2 tablespoons top-of-the-milk
garlic salt	garlic salt
seasoning	seasoning

Wash the peas and soak them overnight in 1 pint of the stock or water.
Cook for about $\frac{3}{4}$ hour in the same water until soft. If necessary add
    more water.
Peel the onion and carrot and cut them into small pieces.
Melt the fat and fry the vegetables for 5 minutes. Add the remaining
    stock and cook until the vegetables are soft.
Strain the peas and vegetables and keep the liquid on one side.
Purée the peas and vegetables (see p. 9) and mix with the liquid.
Season with garlic salt and pepper to taste.
Reheat the soup and before serving add the top of the milk.
NOTE: *This soup burns easily, so it is important to stir it frequently and
to keep the heat low.*

Tomato soup

4 good servings   *Each serving 15 CHO   175 Cals*

1 lb tomatoes	455 g tomatoes
1 small onion	1 small onion
1 oz butter or margarine	30 g butter or margarine
1 lean rasher of bacon	1 lean rasher of bacon
$\frac{3}{4}$ pint water	425 ml water
1 oz cornflour	30 g cornflour
1 tablespoon tomato purée	1 tablespoon tomato purée
7 fl oz milk	200 ml milk
$\frac{1}{2}$ teaspoon fructose	$\frac{1}{2}$ teaspoon fructose
seasoning	seasoning

Peel and slice the onion and tomatoes.

Heat the butter in a saucepan and fry the chopped bacon and onion but do not let the onion brown.

Add the tomatoes, water and seasoning, bring to the boil and simmer in a covered pan for about 25 minutes.

Blend the cornflour with a little water, add to the soup and return to the boil.

Remove the bacon and rub the soup through a sieve.

Return to the pan and add the milk and fructose. Add tomato purée to taste and re-heat but do not boil.

Watercress soup

4 servings   *Each serving 5 CHO   100 Cals*

1 large bunch or 2 small bunches of watercress

1 small onion

½ oz butter or margarine

¾ pint water

7 fl oz milk

1 chicken stock cube

2 heaped teaspoons cornflour

2 fl oz top of the milk

pepper

1 large bunch or 2 small bunches of watercress

1 small onion

15 g butter or margarine

425 ml water

200 ml milk

1 chicken stock cube

2 heaped teaspoons cornflour

55 ml top of the milk

pepper

Throw away the coarse stems and wash and chop the watercress. Set aside a few sprigs for garnishing.

Peel and slice the onion and fry in heated butter until soft. Add the watercress to the pan and continue frying gently for 2 or 3 minutes, turning all the time.

Dissolve the stock cube in boiling water and add to the pan. Cover and simmer for about 25 minutes.

Blend the cornflour with a little of the milk and add with the rest of the milk to the pan.

Cool and reduce to a purée (see p. 9).

Return to the pan.

Bring to the boil and simmer very gently for about 5 minutes, stirring all the time.

Check the seasoning and just before serving stir in the top-of-the-milk and garnish with watercress.

Meat and savoury

Most diet sheets prescribe as a main course an average helping of meat, poultry, fish, eggs or cheese. Diabetics often ask what an average helping is. Usually it is about 4 oz (115 g) of meat, but people on a reducing diet should limit themselves to 2 oz (55 g).

Some diabetics persuade themselves that meat means a cut off the joint or a steak at every meal. In fact, cheaper cuts, mince and some soya products are just as good protein although they do need more preparation.

Diabetics are right to be wary of made-up dishes if they do not know the ingredients, but it is hoped that recipes in this section will show that the main course need not necessarily be a straightforward 'meat and two veg'.

Bacon plate

4 servings   *Each serving 15 CHO   374 Cals*

8 oz boiled bacon (pieces are suitable)

1 oz long-grain rice

1 oz packeted herb stuffing

¼ oz butter or margarne

1 medium onion

1 small green pepper, optional

2 tablespoons tomato purée

2 oz grated Cheddar cheese

1 tablespoon milk

seasoning

225 g boiled bacon (pieces are suitable)

30 g long-grain rice

30 g packeted herb stuffing

10 g butter or margarine

1 medium onion

1 small green pepper, optional

2 tablespoons tomato purée

55 g grated Cheddar cheese

1 tablespoon milk

seasoning

Preheat the oven to 350°F/Mark 4.

Boil the rice until just soft. If the bacon is salty, do not salt the water.

Peel the onion and remove the seeds from the pepper. Mince the vegetables.

Trim any excess fat from the bacon and mince the meat.

Make up the stuffing according to the instructions on the packet and blend in the butter.

Put the minced bacon, onion and pepper in a mixing bowl and add the stuffing, rice, tomato purée and three-quarters of the cheese. Bind with the milk and mix thoroughly. Check the seasoning.

Grease a pie plate or flan tin and press in the mixture to a thickness of about three-quarters of an inch.

Sprinkle with the remaining cheese, cover with foil and bake for 15 to 20 minutes.

Remove the foil and put under a hot grill to brown the cheese lightly before serving.

Serve hot or cold.

Beef stew & dumplings

2 servings   *Each serving 20 CHO   662 Cals*

For the stew:

½ lb stewing steak, trimmed	225 g stewing steak, trimmed
1 medium onion	1 medium onion
2 medium carrots	2 medium carrots
1 small turnip	1 small turnip
stock or water	stock or water
seasoning	seasoning
1 tablespoon cooking oil	1 tablespoon cooking oil

For the dumplings:

2 oz self-raising flour	55 g self-raising flour
1 oz suet	30 g suet
½ level teaspoon baking powder	½ level teaspoon baking powder
a little water	a little water

Cut the steak into chunks and fry it in the heated oil in a heavy
saucepan until lightly browned.

Peel and chop the vegetables and add them to the pan.

Barely cover with stock or water and season to taste.

Cover the pan and simmer very gently for about 1½ hours.

Rub the flour, baking powder and suet together and mix with enough
water to form a sticky dough. Roll out by hand.

Divide the mixture into four dumplings, add to the stew and continue
cooking for 20 minutes.

Braised kidneys

2 lambs' kidneys	2 lambs' kidneys
2 rashers streaky bacon	2 rashers streaky bacon
1 medium onion	1 medium onion
1 stick celery	1 stick celery
½ oz dripping or butter	15 g dripping or butter
8 oz tinned whole tomatoes	225 g tinned whole tomatoes
1 teaspoon mixed herbs	1 teaspoon mixed herbs
seasoning	seasoning

Preheat the oven to 350°F/Mark 4.

Peel and chop the onion. Trim, wash and chop the celery. Skin and core the kidneys, wrap each in a trimmed bacon rasher and arrange in a casserole dish.

Heat the fat and fry the onion and celery until the onion softens.

Drain the surplus juice from the tomatoes and add them with the herbs and seasoning to the pan.

Spoon the vegetable mixture over the kidneys, cover and cook in the oven for about 45 minutes.

Chicken casserole

2 servings   *Each serving 5 CHO   311 Cals*

2 chicken pieces (preferably breasts)

1 medium onion

1 large carrot

2 celery sticks and/or a small turnip

4 oz mushrooms

$\frac{1}{2}$ oz flour

$\frac{1}{4}$ oz butter or margarine

1 tablespoon cooking oil

$\frac{1}{2}$ teaspoon mixed dried herbs

$\frac{1}{2}$ pint chicken stock

seasoning

2 chicken pieces (preferably breasts)

1 medium onion

1 large carrot

2 celery sticks and/or a small turnip

115 g mushrooms

15 g flour

10 g butter or margarine

1 tablespoon cooking oil

$\frac{1}{2}$ teaspoon mixed dried herbs

285 ml chicken stock

seasoning

Preheat the oven to 350°F/Mark 4.

Trim and slice all the vegetables.

Heat the butter and oil in a pan and fry the onions until soft.

Transfer to a casserole.

Skin the chicken pieces, dust with flour and fry in the butter and oil until lightly browned

Add the chicken to the casserole with all other ingredients except the stock.

Pour the stock into the frying pan and stir over a gentle heat to collect any flour and cooking juices. Pour the thickened stock into the casserole.

Check the seasoning and cover the casserole.

Bake for about an hour.

Chicken liver pâté

3 servings

Each serving negligible CHO
234 Cals

¼ lb chicken liver	115 g chicken liver
2 oz streaky bacon rashers or bacon pieces	55 g streaky bacon rashers or bacon pieces
½ oz butter or margarine	15 g butter or margarine
½ teaspoon mixed dried herbs	½ teaspoon mixed dried herbs
crushed clove of garlic or garlic salt, optional	crushed clove of garlic or garlic salt, optional
1 teaspoon brandy or dry sherry, optional	1 teaspoon brandy or dry sherry, optional
seasoning	seasoning

Trim the bacon and cut it into small pieces.

Heat the butter and bacon rinds in a pan and gently fry the bacon, liver, garlic, herbs and seasoning for about 10 minutes turning from time to time.

Remove the rinds and pass the liver and bacon twice through the mincer.

Stir in the alcohol (if used) and chill the pâté in a refrigerator in a small covered jar before serving.

Chicken mushroom – quick recipe

2 servings   *Each serving 5 CHO   232 Cals*

½ small chicken or	½ small chicken or
2 chicken pieces	2 chicken pieces
7 fl oz condensed chicken soup	200 ml condensed chicken soup
2 oz mushrooms	55 g mushrooms
¼ oz butter or oil	10 g butter or oil

Preheat the oven to 375°F/Mark 5.

Paint the chicken with butter or oil and roast in a covered casserole
   for 15 minutes.

Trim and slice the mushrooms and add to the dish. Pour on the
   undiluted soup and bake in a covered dish for 20 to 25 minutes.

Corned beef quickie

1 serving   *Negligible CHO   271 Cals*

2 oz corned beef	55 g corned beef
1 egg	1 egg
1 fl oz milk	30 ml milk
1 oz grated Cheddar cheese	30 g grated Cheddar cheese
pinch mixed herbs	pinch mixed herbs
½ teaspoon made mustard	½ teaspoon made mustard
salt and pepper	salt and pepper

Mash the corned beef with the herbs and a little made mustard, put in a
   small ovenproof dish and place under a moderate grill to heat
   through.

Beat the egg and milk together, add the pepper and salt, and pour over
   the corned beef.

Sprinkle with the grated cheese and cook under the grill until the egg
   has just set and the cheese has lightly browned.

Lamb with apples

4 servings   *Each serving 25 CHO   395 Cals*

4 lamb chops	4 lamb chops
6 small potatoes (sliced)	4 small potatoes (sliced)
2 large onions	2 large onions
½ oz flour	15 g flour
½ pint stock	285 ml stock
3 apples (peeled and sliced)	3 apples (peeled and sliced)
2 oz cheese	55 g cheese
2 teaspoons oil	2 teaspoons oil
salt and pepper	salt and pepper

Preheat the oven to 350°F/Mark 4.

Fry the chops in the oil and remove from the pan. Fry the potatoes and
the onions in the same pan. Put half the potato and onion in the
bottom of a casserole, add the chops and then cover with the rest
of the potatoes and onions.

Add the flour to the fat in the pan, brown it, add the stock to form a
brown sauce and season.

Pour the sauce over the meat and arrange the apples on top.

Bake for 1–1½ hours. Remove from the oven, sprinkle with cheese and
return to the oven for another 10–15 minutes or until the cheese is
golden brown.

Lamb stew

3 servings   *Each serving 5 CHO   335 Cals*

6 small chops	6 small chops
1 medium onion	1 medium onion
2 carrots	2 carrots
1 small turnip	1 small turnip
teaspoon mixed herbs	teaspoon mixed herbs
$\frac{1}{2}$ oz flour	15 g flour
$\frac{3}{4}$ pint stock	425 ml stock
seasoning	seasoning
1 tablespoon oil	1 tablespoon oil

Preheat the oven to 325°F/Mark 3.

Trim excess fat from the chops.

Dust the chops with flour and fry in the heated oil until lightly browned.

Transfer to a casserole and add the trimmed and sliced vegetables, herbs and stock.

Season to taste, cover and cook for about 1½ hours.

Liver & bacon rolls

2 servings   *Each serving nil CHO   530 Cals*

4 oz calves' liver   115 g calves' liver
4 oz bacon (4 bacon rashers)   115 g bacon (4 bacon rashers)
pinch or herbs   pinch of herbs
a little made mustard   a little made mustard
½ oz butter or oil   15 g butter or oil

Cut the liver into 4 strips about 3 in long.

Trim the rinds from the bacon, spread the rashers with the herbs and
mustard and wrap them around the strips of liver.

Secure the rolls with a wooden cocktail stick, threading two rolls on
each stick.

Heat the butter or oil and bacon rinds in a pan and fry the bacon rolls
for about 10 minutes, turning from time to time.

Meat loaf

6 slices   *Each slice negligible CHO*
                             170 Cals

1 rasher bacon, lean	1 rasher bacon, lean
½ lb minced beef	225 g minced beef
½ lb minced pork or veal	225 g minced pork or veal
1 beaten egg	1 beaten egg
2 teaspoons Worcester sauce	2 teaspoons Worcester sauce
2 teaspoons tomato purée	2 teaspoons tomato purée
teaspoon mixed herbs	teaspoon mixed herbs
seasoning	seasoning

Preheat the oven to 325°F/Mark 3.
Chop the bacon finely, mix with the other ingredients, bind with the
    beaten egg and season to taste.
Lightly oil a small bread tin, fill with the mixture and cover with foil.
Bake for 45 minutes. Remove the foil and drain off any excess fat.
Raise the heat to 375°F/Mark 5 and bake for a further 15 minutes.
Cool in the tin before turning out.

Minced meat pie

2 servings   *Each serving 20 CHO   410 Cals*

Pastry:

2 oz flour	55 g flour
1 oz lard or margarine	30 g lard or margarine
1 tablespoon of water	1 tablespoon of water

Filling:

8 oz mince	225 g mince
1 small onion, finely chopped	1 small onion, finely chopped
2 oz mushrooms	55 g mushrooms
1 teaspoon tomato purée	1 teaspoon tomato purée
1 teaspoon mixed herbs	1 teaspoon mixed herbs
3 fl oz stock/water	85 ml stock/water
seasoning	seasoning

Preheat the oven to 375°F/Mark 5.

Make the pastry with the flour, fat and water.

Fry the mince in a dry pan until lightly browned and transfer to a small
pie dish.

Fry the onion in the fat from the mince until soft. Mix with the mince
in the dish.

Slice the mushrooms and add to the mixture.

Mix together the stock, herbs and tomato purée, season to taste and
pour over the mince mixture.

Roll out the pastry and cover the dish.

Bake for about 30 minutes.

Pork chops in cider

2 servings   *Each serving 10 CHO   898 Cals*

2 pork chops
1 sliced onion
$\frac{1}{2}$ oz dripping or cooking oil
1 hard eating apple
5 fl oz dry cider
$\frac{1}{4}$ oz cornflour
1 tablespoon water
seasoning

2 pork chops
1 sliced onion
15 g dripping or cooking oil
1 hard eating apple
140 ml dry cider
10 g cornflour
1 tablespoon water
seasoning

Preheat the oven to 350°F/Mark 4.
Heat the fat, fry the onion until soft and transfer to a casserole.
Peel and slice the apple and fry gently for a few minutes before adding to the onions.
Fry the chops for a minute or two and add to the casserole.
Blend the cornflour with the water to form a smooth paste. Add the cider. Bring to the boil in the frying pan. Pour the sauce into the casserole. Season to taste, cover dish and cook in the oven for about 30 minutes.

Pork roll

4 servings   *Each serving 5 CHO   1219 Cals*

2¼ lb lean belly pork	1 kilo lean belly pork
½ lemon	½ lemon
1 small onion	1 small onion
2 teaspoons fresh chopped mint, sage or parsley	2 teaspoons fresh chopped mint, sage or parsley
1 oz packeted herb stuffing	30 g packeted herb stuffing
oil	oil
seasoning	seasoning

Preheat the oven to 375°F/Mark 5.

Remove the bones from the pork and score the crackling. You may ask your butcher to do this.

Grate the lemon and squeeze out the juice.

Chop the onion and fresh herbs finely.

Make up the stuffing with the water and lemon juice following the instructions on the packet.

Heat a little oil and fry the onion for a few minutes until soft. Blend into the stuffing with the lemon rind and fresh herbs. Season to taste.

Spread the stuffing over the pork and tie in a roll.

Paint the crackling generously with oil and rub with salt.

Bake for 1¼ hours with the meat covered but not enclosed in foil.

Remove the foil, turn the oven up to 425°F/Mark 7, and bake for a further quarter of an hour until the crackling has browned.

Rabbit pie

5 servings   *Each serving 20 CHO   746 Cals*

---

8 oz flaky pastry (bought or made at home with 5 oz flour)	225 g flaky pastry (bought or made at home with 140 g flour)
1 rabbit or 5 rabbit joints	1 rabbit or 5 rabbit joints
4 oz bacon pieces	115 g bacon pieces
1 medium onion	1 medium onion
2 oz dripping	55 g dripping
½ pint stock	285 ml stock
1 teaspoon chopped fresh sage or	1 teaspoon chopped fresh sage or
½ teaspoon dried sage	½ teaspoon dried sage
seasoning	seasoning

Preheat the oven to 350°F/Mark 4.

Cut the rabbit into joints and trim and chop the bacon. Peel and slice the onion and fry in the heated dripping in a large heavy saucepan until soft. Set the onion aside.

Fry the rabbit joints and bacon in the same pan until lightly browned.

Add the onions, sage and stock to the pan, season to taste, cover and simmer gently for about 45 minutes.

Leave to cool before transferring to the pie-dish.

Roll out the pastry and cover the dish.

Bake for about an hour.

Pressed tongue

4 servings

Each serving negligible CHO
515 Cals

1½ lb calves' or lambs' tongues	680 g calves' or lambs' tongues
1 pint water	570 ml water
1 stock cube	1 stock cube
1 small onion	1 small onion
1 carrot	1 carrot
1 bayleaf	1 bayleaf
6 peppercorns	6 peppercorns
salt	salt

Wash the tongues and soak them in salted water for about 2 hours. Drain. Put the tongues in a saucepan with a pint of fresh water, the onion, carrot, bayleaf, peppercorns and stock cube.

Cover the pan, bring to the boil and simmer for about 1½ hours. Lambs' tongues will take a little less than this, calves' tongues may take longer.

To test if the tongues are cooked, pierce with a fork. If they feel tender and the skin can be lifted off easily they are cooked.

Remove from the heat, drain and keep the cooking liquor on one side. While still hot, remove the skin, small bones and gristle at the root of the tongues.

Pack the tongues tightly into a small soufflé dish or round cake tin with the roots in the middle and the tips round the outer edge of the dish.

Strain about half a cup of the cooking liquor over the tongues and cover the dish with foil. Put a heavy weight on the dish and leave in a cool place overnight.

Turn out and serve.

NOTE: *The remaining cooking liquid can be strained and served as soup or used as stock.*

Rissoles

2 servings   *Each serving 20 CHO   372 Cals*

6 oz mince	170 g mince
2 oz bread (without crusts)	55 g bread (without crusts)
1 small onion, finely chopped	1 small onion, finely chopped
2 teaspoons mixed herbs	2 teaspoons mixed herbs
1 beaten egg	1 beaten egg
$\frac{1}{2}$ oz flour	15 g flour
oil for frying	oil for frying
seasoning	seasoning

Soak the bread in water for a few minutes, squeeze out the excess water
   and mix the damp bread with the mince, chopped onion, beaten
   egg, herbs and seasoning.

Knead by hand for about 5 minutes until the ingredients are
   thoroughly blended.

Using a teaspoon, form the mixture into small balls, roll each one in
   flour, flatten slightly and fry for about 3–4 minutes on each side in
   about half an inch of hot oil. When cooked, the balls should be
   brown and crisp.

Drain well on kitchen paper.

NOTE: *These can be eaten hot or cold.*

Sausage & liver pâté

8 slices

Each slice negligible CHO
225 Cals

½ lb calves' or pigs' liver	225 g calves' or pigs' liver
½ lb pork sausage meat	225 g pork sausage meat
1 small onion, finely chopped	1 small onion, finely chopped
bay leaves	bay leaves
1 teaspoon mixed dried herbs	1 teaspoon mixed dried herbs
or	or
2 teaspoons fresh chopped parsley and thyme	2 teaspoons fresh chopped parsley and thyme
garlic salt, optional	garlic salt, optional
1 beaten egg	1 beaten egg
4 oz streaky bacon	115 g streaky bacon
seasoning	seasoning

Preheat the oven to 375°F/Mark 5.

Mince the liver and mix it with the sausage meat and finely chopped onion, herbs and seasoning.

Pass the mixture again through the mincer. Bind with the beaten egg.

Line a deep casserole dish with the trimmed bacon rashers, press in the liver and sausage meat mixture and arrange the bay leaves on top.

Cover the dish with foil, then put on the lid and place in a roasting tin half full of water.

Bake for about 1¼ hours.

Remove from the oven and leave in cool place. When the pâté is quite cold, remove the lid and foil, cover it with greaseproof paper and place a weight on top. Leave for a few hours.

Turn out to serve.

Shepherd's pie

4 servings   *Each serving 25 CHO   371 Cals*

12 oz mince	340 g mince
1 lb potatoes	455 g potatoes
1 small onion	1 small onion
½ oz dripping or cooking oil	15 g dripping or cooking oil
1 teaspoon mixed herbs	1 teaspoon mixed herbs
1 Oxo cube	1 Oxo cube
½ cup of water	½ cup of water
2 fl oz milk	55 ml milk
½ oz butter or margarine	15 g butter or margarine
seasoning	seasoning

Preheat the oven to 375°F/Mark 5.

Boil the potatoes in salted water, drain and mash with the milk and
    butter or margarine.

Fry the onion in the dripping or oil until soft and add the mince. When
    browned, add the herbs, crumble in the Oxo cube and pour on the
    water. Check the seasoning.

Transfer the meat to a pie-dish. Spread the potato evenly on top.

Bake for about 30 minutes.

Smokey snaps flan

8 servings   *Each serving 20 CHO   391 Cals*

Pastry:

7 oz flour	200 g flour
1½ oz margarine	45 g margarine
2 oz lard	55 g lard
2 tablespoons water	2 tablespoons water

Filling:

4 oz Smokey Snaps	115 g Smokey Snaps
2 cups boiling water	2 cups boiling water
1 teaspoon Bovril or Marmite	1 teaspoon Bovril or Marmite
1 onion, minced	1 onion, minced
2 oz grated Cheddar cheese	55 g grated Cheddar cheese
2 beaten eggs	2 beaten eggs
teaspoon mixed herbs	teaspoon mixed herbs
stuffed olives or strips of tomato for decoration, optional	stuffed olives or strips of tomato for decoration, optional
seasoning	seasoning

Preheat the oven to 375°F/Mark 5.

Make the pastry in the usual way using flour, margarine, lard and
water. Roll out thinly and line a 9- or 10-in flan tin.

Make up the Smokey Snaps with 2 cups of boiling water in which the
Bovril or Marmite has been dissolved.

Leave the Smokey Snaps mixture to cool before adding all the other
ingredients and binding with the beaten eggs. Mix well.

Spread the filling in the pastry case and bake for about 25 minutes.

Decorate if liked and serve hot or cold.

Soya curry

3 servings   *Each serving 20 CHO   267 Cals*

15 oz tin Cadbury's Soya Choice Chunks	425 g tin Cadbury's Soya Choice Chunks
1 medium sized onion, chopped	1 medium sized onion, chopped
1 tablespoon oil or butter	1 tablespoon oil or butter
2 oz mushrooms	55 g mushrooms
2 oz chopped apples	55 g chopped apples
2 teaspoons curry powder	2 teaspoons curry powder
5 fl oz water or stock	140 ml water or stock
1 level tablespoon sultanas	1 level tablespoon sultanas

Heat the oil and fry the chopped onion until transparent. Add the sliced mushrooms, chopped apple and curry powder to the pan and fry gently for 2 to 3 minutes.

Add the Soya Chunks, sultanas and stock and cook over a low heat for 20 minutes.

NOTE : *Soya protein contains very little fat and tends to stick to the pan so it is necessary to stir frequently during cooking. A little extra water may be added if the curry appears to be getting dry.*

Soya mince soufflé

4 servings   *Each serving 20 CHO   257 Cals*

15 oz Cadbury's Soya Choice
    Mince (1 tin)

425 g Cadbury's Soya Choice
    Mince (1 tin)

1 medium onion

1 medium onion

tablespoon cooking oil

tablespoon cooking oil

4 oz mushrooms

115 g mushrooms

teaspoon mixed herbs

teaspoon mixed herbs

2 teaspoons tomato purée

2 teaspoons tomato purée

teaspoon Worcester sauce

teaspoon Worcester sauce

pinch of nutmeg, optional

pinch of nutmeg, optional

1 large egg

1 large egg

½ lb mashed potatoes

225 g mashed potatoes

salt and pepper

salt and pepper

Preheat the oven to 375°F/Mark 5.

Peel and slice the onion and prepare and slice the mushrooms.

Heat the oil in a pan and fry the onion until soft. Add the mushrooms
    to the pan and fry for a further few minutes.

Separate the egg and beat the white until stiff.

Combine the Soya Mince, onion, mushrooms, herbs, Worcester sauce,
    tomato purée and nutmeg. Add salt and pepper to taste.

Mash the well-seasoned potatoes with the yolk, adding a little milk if
    necessary, until the potato is soft and smooth. Fold in the stiffly-
    beaten egg white.

Put the Soya Mince mixture into a greased 2-pint soufflé dish and
    spread the potato mixture on top.

Bake for 35 to 45 minutes until golden brown on top.

Spaghetti bolognese

2 servings   *Each serving 25 CHO   584 Cals*

$\frac{3}{4}$ lb mince	340 g mince
1 medium onion, finely sliced	1 medium onion, finely sliced
2 teaspoons oil	2 teaspoons oil
$\frac{1}{2}$ oz butter or margarine	15 g butter or margarine
small green pepper, optional	small green pepper, optional
5 oz tin peeled tomatoes	140 g tin peeled tomatoes
or	or
2 large fresh tomatoes, peeled	2 large fresh tomatoes, peeled
4 oz mushrooms	115 g mushrooms
2 oz spaghetti	55 g spaghetti
1 oz grated Cheddar or Parmesan cheese	30 g grated Cheddar or Parmesan cheese
2 teaspoons tomato purée	2 teaspoons tomato purée
seasoning	seasoning

Fry the mince in a dry pan until lightly browned. Pour off any excess
    fat and set the mince aside. Peel and slice the onion.
De-seed and slice the pepper and wipe and slice the mushrooms.
Heat the oil and butter in a pan and fry the onion and pepper until the
    onion is soft but not browned.
Add the tomatoes, mushrooms, mince and tomato purée to the pan,
    season to taste, and cook gently for 10 to 15 minutes, stirring
    from time to time.
In the meantime bring a large pan of salted water to the boil and cook
    the spaghetti according to the directions on the packet. (About 10
    to 15 minutes.)
Drain the spaghetti well and serve with the bolognese sauce.
Sprinkle with grated cheese just before bringing the dish to the table.

Steak and kidney hotpot

4 servings   *Each serving 25 CHO   480 Cals*

1 lb stewing steak, trimmed	455 g stewing steak, trimmed
½ lb ox kidney, trimmed	225 g ox kidney, trimmed
½ oz flour	15 g flour
1 lb potatoes	455 g potatoes
1 medium onion	1 medium onion
1 oz beef dripping	30 g beef dripping
½ pint beef stock	285 ml beef stock
1 teaspoon Worcester sauce	1 teaspoon Worcester sauce
½ oz butter or margarine	15 g butter or margarine
seasoning	seasoning

Preheat the oven to 300°F/Mark 2.

Cut the beef and kidney into cubes and dust with flour.

Peel and thickly slice the potatoes.

Peel and slice the onion and fry gently in the heated dripping until soft, using a heavy saucepan. Do not allow the onion to brown.

Add the beef and kidney to the pan. Turn up the heat a little and fry until the meat browns.

Pour on the stock, add the Worcester sauce and seasoning and stir until it boils.

Transfer to a casserole dish and arrange the potato slices on top. Brush with melted butter and sprinkle with salt and pepper.

Cover the dish and bake for about 2 hours.

Stuffed heart

2 servings   *Each serving 10 CHO   331 Cals*

1 pig's heart	1 pig's heart
1⅓ oz soft breadcrumbs	40 g soft breadcrumbs
1 level teaspoon thyme	1 level teaspoon thyme
1 level teaspoon parsley	1 level teaspoon parsley
1 small egg, beaten	1 small egg, beaten
4 fl oz water	115 ml water
seasoning	seasoning

Preheat the oven to 375°F/Mark 5.

Prepare the heart by cutting out all the white tubes and washing well to remove any bloodclots.

Chop the onion finely and combine with the breadcrumbs, herbs and seasoning. Bind with the beaten egg.

Put the stuffing in the heart, place in a casserole dish with the water and bake uncovered for about 45 minutes.

Tripe & onions

2 servings   *Each serving 10 CHO   310 Cals*

1 lb dressed tripe	455 g dressed tripe
1 large onion, thinly sliced	1 large onion, thinly sliced
5 fl oz milk	140 ml milk
5 fl oz water	140 ml water
½ oz flour	15 g flour
½ teaspoon salt	½ teaspoon salt
pepper to taste	pepper to taste

Cut the tripe into 3-in squares, put in a saucepan, cover with cold water and bring to the boil. Remove from the heat and pour off the water.

Return the tripe to the pan with the sliced onion, salt and pepper. Pour on the milk and water, bring to the boil and simmer for about 3 hours.

About 20 minutes before the end of the cooking time, mix the flour with a little water, add to the pan and stir in well. Return to the heat and simmer for the final 20 minutes.

Turkey fricassée

4 servings   *Each serving 5 CHO   343 Cals*

1 lb cooked turkey or chicken	455 g cooked turkey or chicken
10 fl oz turkey or chicken stock	285 ml turkey or chicken stock
1 oz flour	30 g flour
1 oz margarine	30 g margarine
1 egg yolk	1 egg yolk
2 teaspoons lemon juice	2 teaspoons lemon juice
2 tablespoons single cream	2 tablespoons single cream
chopped parsley	chopped parsley
seasoning	seasoning

Remove the skin and bones and cut the turkey into chunks.

Make a sauce with the flour, margarine and stock, taking care not to let the roux brown. (See p. 9.)

Allow the sauce to cool.

Beat together the egg yolk, cream and lemon juice and stir into the sauce. Season to taste.

Add the turkey pieces to the pan, return to the boil and simmer very gently for about 5 minutes, stirring all the time.

Garnish with parsley before serving.

Egg and cheese

Eggs are cheap and can be quickly and easily prepared, so it is easy to take them for granted.

Diabetics, including those on reducing diets, are usually recommended to have a cooked breakfast. Eggs are the traditional and most popular fare in this country, but cheese has a place on many Continental breakfast tables and is a good protein with which to start the day. Why not try it for a change? One advantage is that it needs no cooking.

Eggs and cheese are both excellent sources of protein and neither contains carbohydrate, but it is a popular misconception that you can eat cheese freely if you need to lose weight. Most cheeses have a high Calorie value because of their fat content, so if you are overweight you should limit your intake to a 1 oz (30 g) serving and you should not nibble cheese between meals. Cream cheese in particular should be avoided as 1 oz (30 g) contains 232 Calories. Cottage cheese, on the other hand, is low in Calories giving only 33 to the ounce (30 g) which is why it figures in many slimming diets. It can be made more interesting if it is sieved and blended with a little Bovril or Marmite or some chopped chives.

Buck rarebit

1 serving   *10 CHO   459 Cals*

$\frac{2}{3}$ oz bread, toasted	20 g bread, toasted
2 oz grated Cheddar cheese	55 g grated Cheddar cheese
1 egg	1 egg
2 teaspoons milk	2 teaspoons milk
1 teaspoon oil or margarine	1 teaspoon oil or margarine
seasoning	seasoning

Put the egg on to poach and in the meantime heat the oil or margarine
in a small heavy pan. Add the cheese and milk to the pan, season
to taste and stir over a very low heat until the mixture is smooth
and creamy.

Pour the cheese mixture on to the toast and top with the poached egg.

Casserole of cheese and potato

1 serving   *15 CHO   276 Cals*

3 oz potato	85 g potato
1 large or 2 small tomatoes	1 large or 2 small tomatoes
1 small onion	1 small onion
$1\frac{1}{2}$ oz grated Cheddar cheese	45 g grated Cheddar cheese
2 fl oz chicken stock	55 ml chicken stock
salt and pepper	salt and pepper

Preheat the oven to 400°F/Mark 6.

Peel and slice the potato and boil it in salted water for 5 minutes.
Drain.

Peel and slice the onion and tomato.

Lightly oil a fireproof dish and fill it with alternate layers of tomato,
onion, cheese and potato, finishing with a layer of cheese.

Season to taste, pour on the stock and bake for about 35 minutes.

Cauliflower cheese

2 servings   *Each serving 15 CHO   380 Cals*

1 cauliflower	1 cauliflower
1 oz margarine	30 g margarine
1 oz flour	30 g flour
7 fl oz milk	200 ml milk
3 fl oz water	85 ml water
2 oz grated Cheddar cheese	55 g grated Cheddar cheese

Trim the outer leaves, wash the cauliflower and cook it in salted, boiling water for 20 to 30 minutes according to size.

Drain and arrange in a heatproof serving dish.

Make a sauce with the margarine, flour, milk, water and cheese. (See p. 9.) Season to taste and pour over the cauliflower.

If liked, a quarter of the cheese may be kept on one side when making the sauce. It can be sprinkled over the cauliflower and browned under a grill before serving.

Cauliflower cheese (low calorie)

2 servings   *Each serving negligible CHO*
                               210 Cals

1 cauliflower	1 cauliflower
3 oz grated cheese (strong Cheddar)	85 g grated cheese (strong Cheddar)
salt and pepper	salt and pepper

Trim the outer leaves from the cauliflower and cook it in boiling, salted water for 20 to 30 minutes according to size.

Drain and arrange in a shallow heatproof dish.

Sprinkle with pepper (if liked) and grated cheese and place under a hot grill until the cheese is lightly browned and bubbly.

Cheese pudding

2 servings   *Each serving 25 CHO   400 Cals*

4 slices of bread from a small sliced loaf buttered on both sides	4 slices of bread from a small sliced loaf buttered on both sides
7 fl oz milk	200 ml milk
2 oz grated cheese	55 g grated cheese
1 egg	1 egg
$\frac{1}{4}$ teaspoon dried oregano or other herbs	$\frac{1}{4}$ teaspoon dried oregano or other herbs
$\frac{1}{2}$ teaspoon mustard powder	$\frac{1}{2}$ teaspoon mustard powder
salt and pepper	salt and pepper

Preheat the oven to 300°F/Mark 2.

Put two of the bread and butter slices on the bottom of a greased ovenproof dish and sprinkle the cheese over them evenly.

Cover with the remaining bread and butter.

Beat together the eggs, milk, herbs, mustard, salt and pepper and pour over the ingredients in the dish.

Leave to stand for half an hour.

Bake for 30 minutes. Then increase the heat to 325°F/Mark 3 for a further 15 minutes until set firm.

Serve immediately.

Cheese & tomato soufflé

2 servings   *Each serving 10 CHO   465 Cals*

1 oz margarine	30 g margarine
½ oz cornflour	15 g cornflour
5 fl oz tomato juice	140 ml tomato juice
3 egg yolks	3 egg yolks
4 egg whites	4 egg whites
2 oz grated Cheddar cheese	55 g grated Cheddar cheese
½ level teaspoon mustard	½ level teaspoon mustard
black pepper to taste	black pepper to taste
pinch of salt	pinch of salt

Preheat the oven to 375°F/Mark 5.

Grease and prepare a soufflé dish. (See p. 9.)

Heat the margarine gently in a saucepan. Remove from the heat and stir in the cornflour.

Return to the heat and cook the roux very gently for 2 or 3 minutes but do not brown.

Remove from the heat again and add the tomato juice gradually, stirring all the time.

Cook slowly until you get a smooth, thick sauce.

Cool slightly before stirring in the beaten egg yolks, cheese, seasoning and mustard.

Whisk the egg whites until stiff and fold carefully with a metal spoon or palette knife into the mixture.

Pour into the soufflé dish and bake for about 25 minutes on the middle shelf of the oven.

Serve immediately.

Corn bake

4 servings   *Each serving 15 CHO   202 Cals*

6 oz sweetcorn	170 g sweetcorn
7 fl oz milk	200 ml milk
1 oz flour	30 g flour
1 oz butter or margarine	30 g butter or margarine
seasoning	seasoning
2 eggs, separated	2 eggs, separated

Preheat the oven to 350°F/Mark 4.
Cook the sweetcorn in slightly salted boiling water until tender.
Drain it, saving half a cup of the cooking liquid. Add this to the milk.
Make a sauce with the butter, flour and the milk and water mixture.
    (See p. 9.)
Cool the sauce slightly, beat in the egg yolks and mix in the sweetcorn.
Check the seasoning.
Whisk the egg whites until stiff and fold into the mixture.
Bake in a soufflé dish on the middle shelf of the oven for 45 minutes.

Cottage cheese fluffy omelette

1 serving   *Negligible CHO   366 Cals*

2 oz cottage cheese, sieved	55 g cottage cheese, sieved
2 eggs	2 eggs
$\frac{1}{4}$ oz butter or margarine	10 g butter or margarine
teaspoon oil	teaspoon oil
pinch dry mustard	pinch dry mustard
1 teaspoon chopped chives or parsley	1 teaspoon chopped chives or parsley
salt and pepper	salt and pepper

Separate the eggs and blend the yolks with the cheese, herbs and mustard.

Add salt and pepper to taste.

Whisk the egg whites until stiff and fold in with a metal spoon.

Heat the butter and oil in a small, heavy frying pan and cook the omelette until the mixture has just set.

Brown lightly under a hot grill, slide onto a hot plate and eat immediately.

Curried eggs

2 servings   *Each serving 25 CHO   433 Cals*

1½ oz long grain rice	45 g long grain rice
a few button mushrooms	a few button mushrooms
2 rashers streaky bacon	2 rashers streaky bacon
1 small onion	1 small onion
½ oz flour	15 g flour
2 hard-boiled eggs	2 hard-boiled eggs
2 level teaspoons curry powder	2 level teaspoons curry powder
seasoning	seasoning
10 fl oz stock	285 ml stock
½ oz butter or dripping	15 g butter or dripping

Boil the rice in salted water for 20 minutes.

Peel and chop the onion and mushrooms finely.

Remove the bacon rind and cut the bacon into strips.

Heat the fat and fry the onion until golden; add the bacon and mushrooms and fry for a further few minutes.

Mix the flour and curry powder and add to the pan.

Pour on the stock and stir until the sauce thickens.

Simmer for about 2 minutes before checking the seasoning.

Cut the eggs in half, arrange on a warmed serving dish and pour on the curry sauce.

Drain the rice and make a border round the egg mixture.

Egg and anchovy mousse

4 servings

Each serving negligible CHO
155 Cals

7 fl oz aspic jelly	200 ml aspic jelly
4 hard-boiled eggs	4 hard-boiled eggs
1 teaspoon anchovy essence	1 teaspoon anchovy essence
2 teaspoons Worcester sauce	2 teaspoons Worcester sauce
1 teaspoon curry powder, optional	1 teaspoon curry powder, optional
4 fl oz whipping cream or thick tinned cream	115 ml whipping cream or thick tinned cream
cucumber slices for garnishing	cucumber slices for garnishing
salt and pepper	salt and pepper

Make the aspic according to the directions on the packet, stir in the curry powder, and allow to cool but not to set.

Chop the eggs roughly and combine in a bowl with the Worcester sauce, anchovy essence and aspic mixture.

Blend the mixture in a liquidiser or rub through a sieve.

Whip the cream until stiff and fold in. Tinned cream will not need whipping.

Test the seasoning, pour into a mould and leave to set.

Turn out and garnish with cucumber slices.

Egg & cheese flan

4 servings   *Each serving 20 CHO   508 Cals*

For pastry:

4 oz flour	115 g flour
1 oz lard	30 g lard
1 oz margarine	30 g margarine
1 tablespoon water	1 tablespoon water

For filling:

4 hard-boiled eggs	4 hard-boiled eggs
3 oz grated Cheddar cheese	85 g grated Cheddar cheese
4 oz diabetic salad cream	115 g diabetic salad cream
seasoning	seasoning
chopped parsley or chives	chopped parsley or chives

Preheat the oven to 400°F/Mark 6.

Make pastry with the flour, lard, margarine and water and roll out thinly.

Line a 7-in flan tin, prick the base and bake blind for about 15 minutes. Allow to cool.

Shell and chop the eggs, mix them with the grated cheese and bind with the salad cream. Season to taste.

Fill the pastry flan case with the mixture and garnish with parsley or chives.

Leek and cheese bake

2 servings   *Each serving 25 CHO   425 Cals*

1 lb leeks	455 g leeks
1 oz margarine	30 g margarine
7 fl oz milk	200 ml milk
3 fl oz water, for the sauce	85 ml water, for the sauce
1 oz flour	30 g flour
2 oz grated Cheddar cheese	55 g grated Cheddar cheese
salt and pepper	salt and pepper

Preheat the oven to 325°F/Mark 3.

Trim the leeks, wash well, cut into 2-in strips and cook in boiling salted
    water until tender.

Drain and arrange in a casserole dish.

Make a sauce with the margarine, flour, milk, water and cheese. (See
    p. 9.) Season to taste.

Pour the sauce over the leeks and bake for about 10 minutes or until
    golden.

Variation: celery may replace the leeks, in which case the CHO value
    will be only 15 per serving.

Leek and cheese bake (low calorie)

2 servings   *Each serving 25 CHO   220 Cals*

1 lb leeks, trimmed	455 g leeks, trimmed
1 oz flour	30 g flour
3 fl oz water, for the sauce	85 ml water, for the sauce
7 fl oz fresh skimmed or reconstituted dried skimmed milk	200 ml fresh skimmed or reconstituted dried skimmed milk
1½ oz grated cheese (strong Cheddar)	45 g grated cheese (strong Cheddar)
salt and pepper	salt and pepper

Preheat the oven to 350°F/Mark 4.

Wash the leeks well, cut into 2-in lengths, cook until tender in boiling salted water, drain and arrange in a casserole dish.

Make a smooth paste with the flour and water.

Bring the milk to the boil and stir into the paste.

Return the sauce to the pan and re-heat, stirring all the time until it thickens.

Blend in the cheese, check the seasoning and pour over the leeks.

Bake for about 10 minutes.

Macaroni cheese

3 servings   *Each serving 25 CHO   440 Cals*

2 oz macaroni	55 g macaroni
1 oz margarine	30 g margarine
1 oz flour	30 g flour
2 oz grated Cheddar cheese	55 g grated Cheddar cheese
7 fl oz milk	200 ml milk
1 fl oz water	30 ml water
1 small onion	1 small onion
1 rasher bacon, optional	1 rasher bacon, optional
2 oz mushrooms	55 g mushrooms
tablespoon oil	tablespoon oil
seasoning	seasoning
level teaspoon dry mustard, optional	level teaspoon dry mustard, optional

Preheat the oven to 350°F/Mark 4.

Boil the macaroni in salted water for about 15 minutes. Drain.

Make a sauce with the margarine, mustard, flour, milk and water. (See p. 9.)

Blend in the cheese. Check the seasoning.

Chop the onion and mushrooms finely, trim and cut the bacon into small strips and fry in the heated oil until the onion is soft.

Mix the macaroni with the onion, mushroom and bacon mixture and transfer to a lightly greased pie dish or casserole.

Pour on the cheese sauce and bake for about 20 minutes.

Omelettes
Basic recipe

2 servings   *Each serving negligible CHO*
                                240 Cals

---

4 eggs	4 eggs
1½ tablespoons cold water	1½ tablespoons cold water
½ oz butter or cooking oil	15 g butter or cooking oil
seasoning	seasoning

Break the eggs into a bowl and beat well with a fork. Just before
    cooking, add the water, salt and pepper.
Heat a heavy frying pan over a low heat, put in the butter or oil and
    when the fat begins to smoke pour in the egg mixture.
Stir gently.
When just set and the edges can be lifted with a palette knife, fold
    in half and slide onto a hot plate.
Serve immediately.

VARIATIONS:
Use the basic recipe above.

Cheese Omelette   *Negligible CHO   600 Cals*
Scatter 3 oz (85 g) grated cheese on the omelette before folding.

Herb Omelette   *Negligible CHO   240 Cals*
Add a tablespoon of finely chopped mixed fresh herbs or a level
    teaspoon of dried herbs to the basic mixture before cooking.

Mushroom Omelette   *Negligible CHO   245 Cals*
Simmer 2 oz (55 g) prepared sliced mushrooms in a little seasoned milk
    for 5 minutes, drain and scatter the mushrooms onto the omelette
    before folding.

Tomato Omelette   *Negligible CHO   300 Cals*
Peel and slice 2 or 3 tomatoes, fry gently in a teaspoon of oil for about
    2 minutes, season and spread over the omelette before folding.

Omelettes (cont.)
Stuffed omelettes

Use basic recipe

Bacon and Potato Omelette

2 servings   *Each serving 10 CHO   465 Cals*

4 oz boiled potato	115 g boiled potato
1 small onion	1 small onion
2 oz bacon	55 g bacon
$\frac{1}{4}$ oz butter or oil	10 g butter or oil
seasoning	seasoning

Dice the potato finely, slice the onion thinly and cut the bacon into strips.

Melt the butter or oil in a frying pan, add the potatoes, onion and bacon, season and cover the pan.

Cook slowly for about 8 minutes, stirring from time to time. Spoon the mixture over the basic omelette before folding.

Bacon and Croûton Omelette

2 servings   *Each serving 10 CHO   570 Cals*

$1\frac{1}{3}$ oz bread	40 g bread
3 oz bacon	85 g bacon
$\frac{1}{2}$ oz butter or oil	15 g butter or oil

Dice the bread and trim the bacon and cut it into strips.

Fry the bacon gently in a dry pan. Remove from the pan and keep hot.

Add fat to the pan and when hot, fry the bread, turning now and then to ensure the croûtons are lightly browned all over.

Spread the bacon and croûtons over the omelette before folding.

Spanish omelette

2 servings   *Each serving 10 CHO   341 Cals*

4 oz boiled potatoes	115 g boiled potatoes
2 oz mushrooms	55 g mushrooms
1 small onion	1 small onion
1 medium tomato	1 medium tomato
strips of red or green pepper, optional	strips of red or green pepper, optional
½ clove garlic, optional	½ clove garlic, optional
chopped chives or parsley	chopped chives or parsley
½ oz butter or margarine	15 g butter or margarine
1 teaspoon oil	1 teaspoon oil
seasoning	seasoning

Peel and chop the onion and tomato and slice the mushrooms.

Dice the potatoes.

Crush the garlic.

Heat the butter in a pan and fry the onion, garlic and pepper strips until soft.

Add the mushrooms, potato and tomato to the pan and cook for a few more minutes. Season to taste.

Set the mixture aside to keep hot and wipe the pan.

Heat the oil in the pan and pour in half the basic omelette mixture. Lift the edges to prevent sticking.

When the omelette starts to set, spread on the vegetable mixture and pour on the rest of the eggs.

Slip the pan under a hot grill and cook until the omelette is just set.

Sprinkle with chives or parsley before serving.

Pizza

For dough:

½ oz dried or fresh yeast	15 g dried or fresh yeast
1 tablespoon warm water	1 tablespoon warm water
1 teaspoon sugar	1 teaspoon sugar
2 oz butter	55 g butter
5 oz flour	140 g flour
1 egg	1 egg

For filling:

6 large skinned tomatoes or 1 large tin	6 large skinned tomatoes or 1 large tin
1 medium onion	1 medium onion
small tin anchovies, optional	small tin anchovies, optional
12 black olives, optional	12 black olives, optional
clove garlic, optional	clove garlic, optional
2 teaspoons mixed herbs	2 teaspoons mixed herbs
seasoning	seasoning
1 tablespoon oil	1 tablespoon oil
4 oz grated Cheddar cheese or	115 g grated Cheddar cheese or
2 oz grated Parmesan cheese	55 g grated Parmesan cheese

Mix the yeast with a tablespoon of warm water and the sugar. (See p. 146.)

Work the butter into the warmed flour, add the beaten egg and yeast mixture and mix to a dough. Knead for 5 minutes. Cover the dough with a damp cloth and leave in a warm place until it doubles its size. (About 1½ hours).

Preheat the oven to 450°F/Mark 8.

Peel and finely chop the onion and tomato. (If tinned tomatoes are used, drain off the surplus liquid.) Stone the olives.

Heat the oil and fry the onion until soft. Add the tomatoes, crushed
 garlic and herbs and simmer for 5 minutes. Check the seasoning.
Remove the dough from the bowl, roll out very thinly and line two 5-in
 sandwich tins.
Spread the filling on the dough, decorate with anchovies and olives and
 sprinkle with cheese.
Bake for about 15 minutes.
Serve hot or cold.

NOTE: *Instead of anchovies or olives, strips of bacon, ham, green pepper
or sardines and mushrooms may be used. The addition of minced meat or
poultry makes a more substantial meal.*

Polish eggs

1 serving   *Each serving 5 CHO   329 Cals*

1 egg	1 egg
1 small onion	1 small onion
8 oz fresh or tinned tomatoes	225 g fresh or tinned tomatoes
1 oz streaky bacon	30 g streaky bacon
paprika, optional	paprika, optional
2 teaspoons oil	2 teaspoons oil

Trim and chop the onion and bacon. Skin the tomatoes if fresh ones
 are used.
Heat the oil with the bacon trimmings and fry the onion until soft.
If canned tomatoes are used, drain off the liquid.
Add the tomatoes to the pan and cook gently for about 5 minutes.
Add the bacon and the seasoning and continue cooking for a few
 minutes.
Remove the bacon rinds and transfer the mixture to a small heated
 serving dish and keep warm.
Poach the egg, place on the mixture and sprinkle with paprika before
 serving.

Quiche lorraine

4 servings   *Each serving 20 CHO   418 Cals*

Pastry:

4 oz flour	115 g flour
1¼ oz lard	35 g lard
1 oz margarine	30 g margarine
1 tablespoon water	1 tablespoon water
pinch of salt	pinch of salt

Filling:

4 oz cottage cheese	115 g cottage cheese
2 eggs	2 eggs
2 fl oz milk	55 ml milk
2 oz bacon	55 g bacon
1 small onion	1 small onion
1 oz grated Cheddar cheese	30 g grated Cheddar cheese
1 tomato	1 tomato
½ teaspoon made mustard	½ teaspoon made mustard
seasoning	seasoning

Preheat the oven to 350°F/Mark 4.
Make pastry with the flour, lard, margarine, water and a pinch of salt.
     Roll it out and line a greased 8-in flan tin.
Bake blind for about 15 minutes. (See p. 8.)
Sieve the cottage cheese and beat it into the eggs, milk and mustard.
Peel and slice the onion thinly. Remove the rinds and cut the bacon
     into strips.
Heat the oil and bacon rinds in a pan and fry the onion until soft but
     not brown. Add the bacon to the pan and cook for a few more
     minutes and then remove the rinds.
Combine the cottage cheese mixture with the onion and bacon, season
     to taste and pour into the pastry-lined tin.
Peel and slice the tomato and arrange on top.

Sprinkle with grated cheese and bake on the middle shelf of the oven
for about 40 minutes until the flan filling is set and lightly
browned.
Serve hot or cold.

Quick egg florentine

1 serving   *Negligible CHO   270 Cals*

8 oz frozen or fresh spinach	225 g frozen or fresh spinach
1 egg	1 egg
1 oz grated Cheddar cheese	30 g grated Cheddar cheese

If fresh spinach is used, wash well and boil with salt until soft enough
to chop. Frozen spinach should be cooked according to the
instructions on the packet.
Drain the spinach and put in a small heat-proof dish.
Poach the egg lightly, place on the spinach, sprinkle with grated cheese
and place under a hot grill until the cheese is lightly browned.

Scotch eggs

4 eggs   *Each egg 15 CHO   400 Cals*

4 hard-boiled eggs	4 hard-boiled eggs
$\frac{1}{2}$ lb sausage meat	225 g sausage meat
1 teaspoon mixed herbs	1 teaspoon mixed herbs
$\frac{1}{2}$ oz flour	15 g flour
1 oz dry breadcrumbs	30 g dry breadcrumbs
seasoning	seasoning
oil for frying	oil for frying

Remove the shells and roll the eggs in flour.

Mix the herbs and seasoning into the sausage meat. Then, using floured hands, knead it on a floured board and completely wrap each egg.

Dust the eggs with flour and roll in the breadcrumbs.

Deep fry in hot oil until lightly browned all over.

Serve hot or cold.

Stuffed pancakes

2 servings

Each serving (2 pancakes)
25 CHO   372 Cals

2 oz flour	55 g flour
1 egg	1 egg
3½ fl oz milk	100 ml milk
1½ fl oz water	45 ml water
3 oz diced cooked chicken	85 g diced cooked chicken
2 fl oz condensed cream of mushroom soup	55 ml condensed cream of mushroom soup
1 oz grated Cheddar cheese	30 g grated Cheddar cheese
seasoning	seasoning
oil or lard for frying	oil or lard for frying

Preheat oven to 350°F/Mark 4.

Make a batter with the flour, egg, milk and water, add a pinch of salt and leave to stand for at least an hour.

Heat a very little oil or lard in a small, heavy frying pan and make four pancakes browned on one side only.

Mix together the chicken and undiluted soup, check the seasoning and place a quarter of the mixture on the browned side of each pancake.

Roll and place in a lightly greased oven-proof dish.

Sprinkle with cheese and bake for about 15 minutes.

Variations: Cooked ham or flaked fish may replace the chicken.

Fish

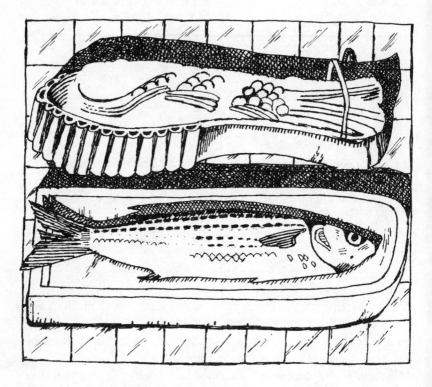

Fish is no longer the cheap substitute for meat it was, but good value can still be had at the fishmongers. Mackerel and coley, for example, compare favourably with meat as an economical source of protein. It is tempting to go for the frozen products and in some places only these are available, but they are more expensive than fresh fish.

White fish is useful to those who need to lose weight because of its low fat content. An ounce of cod or plaice, grilled or steamed, gives only 23 Calories so you can have quite a generous helping (4 oz (115 g)) without adding inches to your waistline.

Young children and people in later life find fish easy to chew and therefore easy to digest.

Baked grey mullet

2 servings   *Each serving 5 CHO   523 Cals*

1 grey mullet (about 1 lb in weight)	1 grey mullet (about 450 g in weight)
2 rashers smoked bacon	2 rashers smoked bacon
$\frac{2}{3}$ oz breadcrumbs	20 g breadcrumbs
4 sage leaves or 1 teaspoon dried sage	4 sage leaves or 1 teaspoon dried sage
$\frac{1}{2}$ oz butter or margarine	15 g butter or margarine

Preheat the oven to 400°F/Mark 6.

Clean and scale the fish and slash in 4 or 5 places on each side.

Chop the bacon and sage leaves finely and mix with the breadcrumbs to make the stuffing.

Press the stuffing into the belly cavity of the mullet and top each slash mark with a knob of butter.

Wrap the fish in foil and bake for 30 minutes.

Place under a hot grill for a few minutes to brown lightly before serving.

Coley casserole

2 servings   *Each serving 15 CHO   393 Cals*

½ lb coley	225 g coley
4 oz onions	115 g onions
4 oz tomatoes	115 g tomatoes
4 oz mushrooms	115 g mushrooms
7 fl oz milk	200 ml milk
½ oz flour	15 g flour
½ oz margarine	15 g margarine
1 oz grated Cheddar cheese	30 g grated Cheddar cheese
¼ teaspoon mustard, optional	¼ teaspoon mustard, optional
tablespoon cooking oil	tablespoon cooking oil
bay leaf	bay leaf
seasoning	seasoning

Preheat the oven to 350°F/Mark 4.

Poach the coley in the milk with the bay leaf. Remove and discard the skin and bones.

Strain and keep the milk. Flake the fish.

Peel and slice the onions, tomatoes and mushrooms.

Heat the oil and fry the onions until soft.

Grease a casserole dish and fill it with alternate layers of onion, fish, tomatoes and mushrooms.

Make a sauce with the margarine, flour and mustard.

Add half the cheese to the sauce and cook for a few minutes until well blended.

Season to taste and pour over the ingredients in the casserole.

Sprinkle the remaining cheese on top and bake for about 25 minutes until the cheese is browned.

Fish cakes

4 servings, 8 cakes

2 cakes contain 15 CHO
244 Cals

12 oz seabream or other white fish	340 g seabream or other white fish
*10 oz peeled old potatoes	*285 g peeled old potatoes
2 oz grated Cheddar cheese	55 g grated Cheddar cheese
$\frac{2}{3}$ oz breadcrumbs	20 g breadcrumbs
1 teaspoon anchovy essence, optional	1 teaspoon anchovy essence, optional
1 teaspoon mixed herbs	1 teaspoon mixed herbs
1 tablespoon cooking oil	1 tablespoon cooking oil
seasoning	seasoning

Poach the fish in salted water. Skin and remove the bones and flake the
fish.

Boil the potatoes, mash them and while they are still hot blend in the
cheese, beating with a wooden spoon until smooth.

Mix in the fish, herbs, anchovy essence and seasoning to taste.

Roll by hand into 8 cakes and dust with the breadcrumbs.

These cakes are improved by being chilled for an hour or two before
being fried in heated oil.

* *Instant mashed potato may be used, made up according to the
maker's instructions.*

Fish flan

4 servings   *Each serving 20 CHO   430 Cals*

Pastry:

4 oz flour	115 g flour
1½ oz cooking fat	45 g cooking fat
1 oz margarine	30 g margarine
pinch salt	pinch salt
water to mix	water to mix

Filling:

6 oz cooked or tinned fish, flaked	170 g cooked or tinned fish, flaked
1 large tomato	1 large tomato
1 medium onion	1 medium onion
4 fl oz milk	115 ml milk
1 large or 2 small eggs	1 large or 2 small eggs
1 oz grated cheese	30 g grated cheese
½ oz butter	15 g butter
seasoning	seasoning

Preheat the oven to 375°F/Mark 5.

Make the pastry in the usual way, roll out thinly and line a 7-in pie
    plate.

Prick the base and bake blind for about 10 minutes. (See p. 8.)

Peel and slice the onion thinly. Peel and chop the tomato.

Melt the butter in a heavy pan and fry the onion until soft and golden.

Arrange the fish, onion and tomato in the flan case.

Beat the eggs and milk together, season and pour into the flan. Sprinkle
    with grated cheese.

Bake for 25 to 30 minutes or until set and golden.

Fish pie

4 servings   ***Each serving 20 CHO   34 Cals***

¾ lb cod or other white fish

2 hard-boiled eggs

4 oz peeled and sliced tomatoes

7 fl oz milk

1 oz margarine or butter

1 oz flour

2 teaspoons chopped parsley or
   1 teaspoon dried herbs

½ lb mashed potato

seasoning

340 g cod or other white fish

2 hard-boiled eggs

115 g peeled and sliced tomatoes

200 ml milk

30 g margarine or butter

30 g flour

2 teaspoons chopped parsley or
   1 teaspoon dried herbs

225 g mashed potato

seasoning

Preheat the oven to 375°F/Mark 5.

Make the milk up to half a pint with water, add salt and pepper and
   poach the fish until the flesh leaves the skin and bones. Keep the
   cooking liquid on one side.

Flake the fish into a fireproof dish, add the sliced egg and the peeled
   and sliced tomatoes.

Make a sauce with the cooking liquid, flour and two-thirds of the
   margarine. (See p. 9.)

Add the herbs, check the seasoning and pour the sauce over the
   ingredients in the dish.

Spread on the mashed potato and dot with the remaining margarine.

Bake for about 15 minutes or until golden brown.

Fish souffle

4 servings   *Each serving 10 CHO   405 Cals*

12 oz whiting or other white fish fillets	340 g whiting or other white fish fillets
7 fl oz milk	200 ml milk
2 oz margarine	55 g margarine
1½ oz flour	45 g flour
4 egg yolks	4 egg yolks
5 egg whites	5 egg whites
1 oz grated Parmesan cheese or strong Cheddar cheese	30 g grated Parmesan cheese or strong Cheddar cheese
2 teaspoons lemon juice	2 teaspoons lemon juice
1 teaspoon anchovy essence, optional	1 teaspoon anchovy essence, optional
1 tablespoon chopped parsley or 2 teaspoons dried herbs	1 tablespoon chopped parsley or 2 teaspoons dried herbs
½ teaspoon mustard, optional	½ teaspoon mustard, optional
seasoning	seasoning

Preheat the oven to 375°F/Mark 5.

Poach the fish in the milk made up to ½ pint with water until it can be skinned and flaked. Strain off the liquid and keep on one side. Discard the skin and bones.

Make a sauce with the flour, margarine, mustard and the cooking liquid. (See p. 9.)

Remove from the heat and beat in the egg yolks one at a time.

Beat in the flaked fish, lemon juice, anchovy essence, herbs and grated cheese.

Season to taste.

Whisk the egg whites until stiff and fold into the mixture.

Pour into a lightly greased 3-pint soufflé dish and bake for 35 to 40 minutes until the soufflé is well risen and golden brown.

Serve immediately.

Fried fish in batter

4 servings   *Each serving 10 CHO   174 Cals*

4 fish fillets (about	4 fish fillets (about
4 oz each)	115 g each)
2 oz flour	55 g flour
1 egg	1 egg
3 fl oz milk	85 ml milk
seasoning	seasoning
oil for frying	oil for frying

Dust the fish with flour.

Put the remaining flour into a bowl, break the egg over it and add half
the milk.

Beat until smooth.

Add the rest of the milk and seasoning and beat again and then coat
the fillets with the batter.

Fry, preferably in very hot deep fat, on both sides until golden brown.

Garnished mackerel

2 servings   *Each serving 5 CHO   325 Cals*

1 lb filleted mackerel	455 g filleted mackerel
2 oz mushrooms	55 g mushrooms
1 small onion	1 small onion
1 teaspoon dried mixed herbs	1 teaspoon dried mixed herbs
1 clove garlic or garlic salt, optional	1 clove garlic or garlic salt, optional
$\frac{1}{4}$ oz flour	10 g flour
1 tablespoon vinegar	1 tablespoon vinegar
2 tablespoons oil	2 tablespoons oil
salt and pepper	salt and pepper

Preheat the oven to 275°F/Mark 1.

Peel and chop the onion and garlic finely and wipe and slice the mushrooms.

Wash and dry the fish fillets and roll them in the flour.

Heat half the oil and fry the mackerel on both sides until brown, then place in a fireproof dish and keep warm in a low oven.

Clean the pan, heat the remaining oil and fry the onion until soft. Add the mushrooms, herbs, garlic and seasoning and continue frying gently for a further 5 minutes.

Pour the vinegar into the pan, bring the mixture to the boil and spread over the fish in the serving dish.

Haddock and egg flan

4 servings   *Each serving 20 CHO   456 Cals*

For the pastry:

4 oz plain flour	115 g plain flour
1 oz lard	30 g lard
1 oz margarine	30 g margarine
1 tablespoon of water	1 tablespoon of water

For the filling:

8 oz cooked smoked haddock	225 g cooked smoked haddock
4 fl oz soured cream	115 ml soured cream
3 hard-boiled eggs	3 hard-boiled eggs
seasoning	seasoning
chopped parsley	chopped parsley

Preheat the oven to 375°F/Mark 5.

Make the pastry in the usual way with the flour, lard, margarine and
water (see p. 14).

Roll out thinly and line a 7-in greased flan tin. Bake blind for 20
minutes (see p. 8).

Remove the skin and bones and flake the fish.

Shell and chop the eggs and mix with the haddock and soured cream.

Check the seasoning and, if possible, chill the mixture for a few hours
before filling the pastry case.

Sprinkle with chopped parsley before serving.

95

Kipper kedgeree

2 servings   *Each serving 20 CHO   407 Cals*

7 oz filleted kipper   200 g filleted kipper
2 oz long grain rice   55 g long grain rice
1 hard-boiled egg   1 hard-boiled egg
½ oz butter or margarine   15 g butter or margarine
2 teaspoons chopped parsley   2 teaspoons chopped parsley
seasoning   seasoning

Cook the kipper in a little water until the skin and any bones can be
    removed and the fish can be flaked.
Add the rice to a pan of boiling, salted water and cook for 15 to 20
    minutes until just tender. Drain.
Combine the rice, chopped egg and flaked kipper, add the butter, check
    the seasoning and serve sprinkled with parsley.
If the kedgeree is to be served cold with salad, leave out the butter and
    mix in 2 teaspoons of French dressing instead.

NOTE: *A 7-oz can of tuna fish can replace the kipper. In this case the
Calorie value of each serving will be 557.*

Plaice florentine

2 servings   *Each serving 10 CHO   320 Cals*

2 plaice fillets

½ lb fresh spinach or a small
    packet of chopped frozen
    spinach

4 fl oz milk

⅓ oz cornflour

2 oz grated Cheddar cheese

seasoning

2 plaice fillets

225 g fresh spinach or a small
    packet of chopped frozen
    spinach

115 ml milk

10 g cornflour

55 g grated Cheddar cheese

seasoning

Preheat the oven to 350°F/Mark 4.

If fresh spinach is used, wash well and boil with a pinch of salt but
    without added water until soft enough to chop. Drain well and
    place on the bottom of a lightly greased oven-proof dish.

Arrange the fish fillets on the spinach with the dark side down.

Mix the cornflour with a little of the milk, bring the rest of the milk to
    the boil, add the cornflour and stir until the sauce thickens and
    clears.

Stir in half the grated cheese and cook for a further few minutes until
    blended.

Check the seasoning, pour the sauce over the fish, sprinkle with the
    remaining cheese and bake for about 15 minutes.

Sardine & cheese puffs

2 servings   *Each serving 10 CHO   573 Cals*

2 eggs	2 eggs
2 oz grated cheese	55 g grated cheese
1½ oz breadcrumbs	45 g breadcrumbs
2 fl oz milk	55 ml milk
4 oz sardines (average tin)	115 g sardines (average tin)
½ oz butter	15 g butter
seasoning	seasoning
tablespoon cooking oil	tablespoon cooking oil

Drain the oil from the sardines and remove the tails and backbones.

Separate the eggs and mix the yolks with the cheese, breadcrumbs and milk.

Melt the butter, stir in well and leave for 5 minutes.

Whisk the egg whites until stiff, fold into the mixture and season to taste.

Heat the oil in a frying pan, cook the mixture for about 3 minutes over a low heat and slide onto a shallow heatproof dish.

Arrange the sardines on the puff and heat under a hot grill.

Sardine pâté

3 servings   *Each serving nil CHO   315 Cals*

4½ oz sardines tinned in oil
   (average tin)

1½ oz cottage cheese, sieved

2 teaspoons fresh lemon juice

black pepper

slices of lemon

130 g sardines tinned in oil
   (average tin)

45 g cottage cheese, sieved

2 teaspoons fresh lemon juice

black pepper

slices of lemon

Drain and discard the oil and remove the tails and spines from the
   sardines.
Put the fish, cheese, lemon juice and pepper in a mixing bowl.
Blend thoroughly with a wooden spoon.
Chill before use and serve with lemon slices.

Savoury custard

2 servings   *Each serving 5 CHO   239 Cals*

---

6 oz cooked white fish

2 eggs

7 fl oz milk

a few button mushrooms,
   optional

seasoning

1 tomato

170 g cooked white fish

2 eggs

200 ml milk

a few button mushrooms,
   optional

seasoning

1 tomato

Preheat the oven to 325°F/Mark 3.
Peel and slice the tomato and slice the mushrooms.
Arrange the vegetables on the bottom of a small oven-proof dish.
Beat together the eggs and milk. Flake the fish and mix it in.
Season to taste and pour over the vegetables in the dish.
Bake for about 25 minutes until the custard has set.
Variations: Grated cheese or diced cooked chicken or ham can replace
   the fish. Any 'free' vegetable can replace the mushrooms.

Soused mackerel

2 servings   *Each serving nil CHO   250 Cals*

2 medium-sized mackerel	2 medium-sized mackerel
6 fl oz vinegar	170 ml vinegar
1 bayleaf	1 bayleaf
6 peppercorns	6 peppercorns
6 whole allspice	6 whole allspice
parsley or fennel	parsley or fennel
pinch of cayenne pepper	pinch of cayenne pepper
salt	salt

Wash and clean the mackerel, put them in a stewpan and cover with
cold water.

Add half a teaspoon of salt and 2 tablespoons of the vinegar, bring
gently to the boil and simmer for 5 minutes over a low heat.

Remove from the heat, pour off the liquid and, when the mackerel has
cooled, take out the backbone. Return to the pan with half a pint
of water, cayenne, spices and the remaining vinegar.

Bring to the boil slowly and simmer gently for a further 10 minutes.

Transfer to a serving dish, pour on the cooking liquid and leave the fish
to steep in this until needed.

Just before serving sprinkle with chopped parsley or fennel.

Tuna fish salad

4 servings   *Each serving negligible CHO*
                                                202 Cals

7 oz tinned tuna fish	200 g tinned tuna fish
3 hard-boiled eggs	3 hard-boiled eggs
2 spring onions	2 spring onions
2 fl oz low calorie mayonnaise	55 ml low calorie mayonnaise
lettuce leaves	lettuce leaves
slices of tomato and cucumber	slices of tomato and cucumber
seasoning	seasoning

Drain and discard the oil and flake the fish into a mixing bowl.

Shell and chop the eggs, slice the onions finely, mix with the fish and
    bind with the mayonnaise. Add seasoning to taste.

The mixture improves when chilled for a few hours.

Arrange on a serving dish and decorate with the lettuce leaves and
    cucumber and tomato slices.

Vegetables

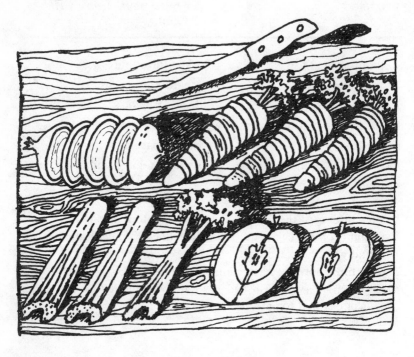

People can be put off vegetables for a lifetime by the way they are served at school dinners. This is a pity as they are essential in a balanced diet and contain vital vitamins and minerals.

Salads and vegetables add colour and have the added advantage of making meat go further.

When you develop diabetes, you may have to rethink your eating pattern. If you have been shunning vegetables you may be agreeably surprised to find that, thanks to refrigeration and better marketing, there is a good variety throughout the year and ways of cooking them that are a long way from the watery and stringy vegetables of unhappy memory.

Nearly all vegetables, with the exception of potatoes, peas, carrots and pulses are low in carbohydrate and Calories and indeed most green vegetables are 'free foods'. You can therefore fill your plate with them when you are hungry.

Apple & celery salad

2 servings   *Each serving 10 CHO 70 Cals*

8 oz dessert apples
    (2 medium sized)

1 tablespoon lemon juice

4 fl oz water

2 sticks celery

$\frac{3}{4}$ oz diabetic salad cream
    (1 level tablespoon)

chopped parsley or chives
    or

$\frac{1}{2}$ teaspoon paprika

225 g dessert apples
    (2 medium sized)

1 tablespoon lemon juice

115 ml water

2 sticks celery

20 g diabetic salad cream
    (1 level tablespoon)

chopped parsley or chives
    or

$\frac{1}{2}$ teaspoon paprika

Mix together the water and lemon juice.

Trim and cut the celery into small strips.

Peel and slice the apples and steep them in the lemon juice and water
    for half an hour. Drain and mix with the celery.

Dress with the salad cream and garnish with parsley, chives or paprika.

Brown lentil stew

4 servings   *Each serving 25 CHO   274 Cals*

7 oz brown lentils (not red)	200 g brown lentils (not red)
1 medium carrot	1 medium carrot
$\frac{1}{2}$ stick celery	$\frac{1}{2}$ stick celery
1 large onion	1 large onion
$1\frac{1}{2}$ oz fat or dripping	45 g fat or dripping
$\frac{1}{2}$ oz flour	15 g flour
$\frac{1}{4}$ pt stock or water	140 ml stock or water
chopped parsley	chopped parsley
salt to taste	salt to taste

Soak the lentils overnight in twice as much water as is necessary to cover them. In the morning transfer the lentils and water to a pan, bring them to the boil and simmer for $1\frac{1}{2}$ hours.

Drain off surplus water.

Melt the fat in a large pan and add the finely chopped vegetables. Fry them gently for a few minutes before adding the flour. Pour on the stock and cook until the vegetables are soft. Check the seasoning.

Add the lentils and reheat the stew.

Serve with chopped parsley.

Corn, ham and cheese supper

2 servings   *Each serving 20 CHO   388 Cals*

6 oz sweetcorn	170 g sweetcorn
2 oz ham or bacon	55 g ham or bacon
2 oz mushrooms	55 g mushrooms
2 oz grated Cheddar cheese	55 g grated Cheddar cheese
1 small onion	1 small onion
2 medium tomatoes	2 medium tomatoes
1 oz butter or oil	30 g butter or oil
seasoning	seasoning

Cook the corn in boiling, salted water until tender.

Peel and chop the onion and tomatoes and slice the mushrooms.

Cut the ham into strips.

Heat the fat in a pan and fry the onions until soft. Then add the mushrooms, tomatoes and ham and continue frying gently until everything is cooked through.

Drain the corn and add it to the pan, check the seasoning and mix well.

Transfer the mixture to a shallow heatproof dish, sprinkle with grated cheese and place under a hot grill until the cheese is browned.

Green peppers, stuffed

2 servings   *Each serving 10 CHO 225 Cals*

2 small green peppers
2 oz boiled rice
   (2 heaped tablespoons)
2 oz bacon rashers
4 oz mushrooms
1 teaspoon oil
garlic salt, optional
seasoning

2 small green peppers
55 g boiled rice
   (2 heaped tablespoons)
55 g bacon rashers
115 g mushrooms
1 teaspoon oil
garlic salt, optional
seasoning

Preheat the oven to 350°F/Mark 4.

Remove the stalks from the peppers so they will stand on their bases, cut off the tops and remove the seeds taking care to keep the shells whole.

Parboil the peppers and their tops in salted water for about 5 minutes. Drain them.

Remove the rind from the bacon, wipe and slice the mushrooms.

Heat the oil and fry the mushrooms and bacon for about 5 minutes. Add the rice to the pan and fry everything together gently for a further minute or two, stirring all the time. Season to taste.

Fill the peppers with the rice mixture, replace the tops and put in a greased casserole.

Cover the dish and bake for 15 to 20 minutes.

Haricot beans with tomatoes

4 servings   *Each serving 25 CHO   224 Cals*

8 oz white beans	225 g white beans
8 oz tin of tomatoes	225 g tin of tomatoes
1 medium onion	1 medium onion
1 oz dripping or oil	30 g dripping or oil
1 clove of garlic, optional	1 clove of garlic, optional
chopped parsley	chopped parsley
seasoning	seasoning

Soak the beans overnight in water, allowing twice the depth of water to beans. Bring them to the boil in the water in which they have been soaking, and simmer for 2 to 3 hours or pressure cook for 30 minutes.

Peel and slice the onion and fry it in the heated fat until it is soft. Add the crushed garlic and tomatoes to the pan and cook gently for 5 minutes.

Combine the onion and tomato mixture with the beans, add seasoning, heat through and serve sprinkled with parsley.

Italian courgettes

4 servings

Each serving negligible CHO
80 Cals

1 lb courgettes/marrow	455 g courgettes/marrow
1 medium onion	1 medium onion
8 oz tin tomatoes or 2 large fresh tomatoes	225 g tin tomatoes or 2 large fresh tomatoes
1 crushed garlic clove or garlic salt, optional	1 crushed garlic clove or garlic salt, optional
½ oz butter or margarine	15 g butter or margarine
1 tablespoon oil	1 tablespoon oil
seasoning	seasoning

Wash, top and tail the courgettes but do not peel them. Cut them into ½-in slices. If marrow is used, peel and chop into 1-in pieces.

Peel and slice the onion and tomato.

Crush the garlic.

Heat the butter and oil and fry the onion and garlic until soft, add the tomatoes to the pan and cook gently for a few minutes, stirring all the time.

Add the courgettes and seasoning and cover the pan.

Simmer gently for about 45 minutes, shaking the pan from time to time to prevent sticking.

NOTE: *To make a light supper dish, put the vegetables in a shallow fireproof dish, sprinkle with 2 oz (55 g) grated cheese and brown under a hot grill. This will increase the Calorie value of each serving to 140.*

Jacket potatoes, stuffed

2 servings   *Each serving 25 CHO   420 Cals*

10 oz old potatoes	285 g old potatoes
(2 medium sized)	(2 medium sized)
4 oz corned beef	115 g corned beef
1 oz margarine or butter	30 g margarine or butter
½ teaspoon made mustard	½ teaspoon made mustard
1 oz grated Cheddar cheese	30 g grated Cheddar cheese
salt and pepper	salt and pepper

Preheat the oven to 350°F/Mark 4.

Wash the potatoes, rub the skins with a little oil and prick them.

Bake for about an hour until tender.

Cut the potatoes in half lengthways, scoop out the centres and mash
    with the corned beef, margarine, mustard and seasoning.

Return the mixture to the jackets, sprinkle with the cheese and place
    under a hot grill until the cheese is lightly browned and bubbling.

Marrow, stuffed

4 servings 　　　　　　　　*Each serving negligible CHO*
　　　　　　　　　　　　　　　320 Cals

1 young marrow (about 1½ lb)	1 young marrow (about 850 g)
1 lb mince	455 g mince
1 medium onion	1 medium onion
4 oz mushrooms	115 g mushrooms
1 oz streaky bacon (2 rashers)	30 g streaky bacon (2 rashers)
1 small green pepper, optional	1 small green pepper, optional
2 teaspoons oil	2 teaspoons oil
1 tablespoon tomato purée	1 tablespoon tomato purée
1 level teaspoon dried herbs seasoning	1 level teaspoon dried herbs seasoning

Preheat the oven to 375°F/Mark 5.

Peel the marrow, cut it in half lengthways and scoop out the seed and pith. Then cut it across to make 4 boats.

Peel and slice the onion thinly, wipe and slice the mushrooms and trim and chop the bacon into strips. De-seed and chop the green pepper.

Brown the mince lightly in a dry frying pan, drain off the fat and set the meat aside.

Heat the oil in the pan and fry the onion and green pepper until the onion is soft but not brown. Add the mushroom and bacon and fry for 2-3 minutes.

Combine the mince, onion and green pepper mixture, herbs and tomato purée and season to taste. Mix well and fill the marrow boats with the mixture.

Wrap the boats in foil and bake in the top half of the oven for about 30 minutes.

Mixed salad

2 servings   *Each serving negligible CHO*
                                44 Cals

2 oz beetroot, cooked	55 g beetroot, cooked
2 medium tomatoes	2 medium tomatoes
slices of cucumber	slices of cucumber
lettuce leaves and/or watercress, chopped celery, chicory, Chinese cabbage	lettuce leaves and/or watercress, chopped celery, chicory, Chinese cabbage

Sprinkle the cucumber slices with salt, leave for half an hour and then
    drain.
Wash and dry the other ingredients.
Arrange all the ingredients in a salad bowl or on two side plates.

Ormskirk slaw

4 servings   *Each serving negligible CHO*
                                25 Cals

1 lb white cabbage	455 g white cabbage
4 oz natural low fat yoghurt	115 g natural low fat yoghurt
2 teaspoons wine vinegar	2 teaspoons wine vinegar
seasoning	seasoning

Remove the core, tough stems and outer leaves of the cabbage. Shred
    the remaining cabbage leaves finely.
Wash the drain the cabbage and put it in a saucepan with the vinegar
    and seasoning.
Boil briskly for 5 minutes, stirring all the time.
Drain, transfer to a hot serving dish and dress with the yoghurt.

Onions, stuffed

2 servings   *Each serving 5 CHO   225 Cals*

2 large Spanish onions	2 large Spanish onions
2 oz mince	55 g mince
1 oz bacon (1 rasher)	30 g bacon (1 rasher)
½ oz packet herb stuffing	15 g packet herb stuffing
½ oz butter or dripping	15 g butter or dripping
seasoning	seasoning

Preheat the oven to 350°F/Mark 4.

Peel the onions and boil them in salted water for about 10 minutes. Drain and cool.

With a sharp knife cut out the centres and chop them finely.

Trim and chop the bacon and fry it gently in a dry pan for a minute or two.

Add the mince and onion centres to the pan and fry for a further few minutes until the mince is lightly browned.

Make up the stuffing according to the directions on the packet, add to the mince mixture, season to taste and fill the onion shells.

Put a small knob of butter or dripping on each onion and bake in a covered dish for about half an hour until the onions are soft.

Pease pudding

4 servings   *Each serving 15 CHO   174 Cals*

4 oz dried peas	115 g dried peas
1 oz butter or margarine	30 g butter or margarine
1 egg	1 egg
salt and pepper	salt and pepper

Wash the peas well before putting them to soak. Leave them to soak
   overnight in twice as much water as is necessary to cover them.
In the morning transfer the peas to a pan, add salt to taste and bring to
   the boil. Simmer for $\frac{3}{4}$ hour in a covered pan (20 minutes in a
   pressure cooker). While simmering, remove any scum that comes
   to the surface. Refrain from adding extra water but stir frequently
   to see the peas do not stick.
When they are cooked, rub the peas through a sieve and beat the purée
   with the margarine and egg. Place in a greased basin and steam for
   half an hour.

Potato salad

4 servings   *Each serving 10 CHO   113 Cals*

8 oz small potatoes	225 g small potatoes
1 tablespoon French dressing	1 tablespoon French dressing
1 tablespoon diabetic salad cream	1 tablespoon diabetic salad cream
salt	salt
paprika or chopped parsley	paprika or chopped parsley

Boil the potatoes in their skins and peel them as soon as they are cool.
Dice them and, while warm, turn the cubes in the French dressing. Add
   salt to taste.
Leave to cool and, just before serving, coat with mayonnaise and
   sprinkle with paprika and/or parsley.

Pilaff rice

3 servings   *Each serving 25 CHO   165 Cals*

3 oz long grain rice   85 g long grain rice
5 fl oz chicken stock   140 ml chicken stock
1 small onion   1 small onion
½ oz butter or margarine   15 g butter or margarine
2 teaspoons oil   2 teaspoons oil
seasoning   seasoning

Preheat the oven to 325°F/Mark 3.
Rinse the rice in cold water and strain.
Heat the butter and oil and fry the onion until soft.
Add the rice to the pan and continue frying until it begins to take
    colour, stirring all the time.
Pour on the hot, seasoned stock, put in a casserole dish, cover and cook
    in the oven until the stock is absorbed and the rice is tender but
    not dry (about 15 to 20 minutes).

Potato bake

2 servings   *Each serving 25 CHO   438 Cals*

8 oz boiled potatoes   225 g boiled potatoes
2 oz bacon rashers   55 g bacon rashers
1 medium onion   1 medium onion
6 fl oz condensed mushroom   170 ml condensed mushroom
   soup   soup
1 fl oz milk   30 ml milk
2 oz grated cheese   55 g grated cheese
seasoning   seasoning

Preheat the oven to 450°F/Mark 7.
Slice the potatoes. Trim and chop the bacon. Peel and slice the onion.
Fry the bacon and when the fat runs, add the onion to the pan and
   cook gently until soft.
Grease a fireproof dish and put in half the potato slices to form a layer.
Spread with the bacon and onion and top with the remaining potato
   slices.
Mix the soup with the milk and three-quarters of the cheese and stir
   over a very gentle heat until the cheese is blended in.
Season to taste and pour over the ingredients in the dish.
Sprinkle with the remaining cheese and bake for 15 to 20 minutes.

Spinach soufflé

4 servings   *Each serving 10 CHO   328 Cals*

3 egg yolks	3 egg yolks
4 egg whites	4 egg whites
8 oz fresh spinach	225 g fresh spinach
1½ oz flour	45 g flour
1½ oz butter or margarine	45 g butter or margarine
½ pint milk	285 ml milk
2 oz grated Cheddar cheese	55 g grated Cheddar cheese
salt and pepper	salt and pepper

Preheat the oven to 400°F/Mark 6.

Trim the spinach, wash it well and cook in just enough salted water to prevent it sticking to the pan.

Drain and reduce it to a wet purée using a little of the cooking water if necessary. Prepare a medium-sized soufflé dish. (See p. 9.)

Make a sauce with flour, butter, milk and cheese. (See p. 9.) Allow to cool.

Separate the eggs and beat the yolks into the sauce.

Then add the spinach purée. Mix well, adding salt and pepper to taste.

Whisk the 4 egg whites until stiff and fold them into the mixture.

Bake for about 35 minutes in the middle of the oven until the soufflé has risen.

Serve immediately.

Tomatoes, stuffed

2 servings   *Each serving 5 CHO   30 Cals*

4 medium tomatoes	4 medium tomatoes
1 small onion or a shallot	1 small onion or a shallot
2 oz mushrooms	55 g mushrooms
½ oz soft white breadcrumbs	15 g soft white breadcrumbs
2 teaspoons fresh chopped parsley or mixed herbs or	2 teaspoons fresh chopped parsley or mixed herbs or
1 teaspoon dried mixed herbs	1 teaspoon dried mixed herbs
tablespoon of oil	tablespoon of oil
seasoning	seasoning

Preheat the oven to 350°F/Mark 4.

Wash the tomatoes, cut off the tops, remove the cores and scoop out the seeds without damaging the shells.

Peel and chop the onion finely and wipe and slice the mushrooms.

Heat the oil and fry the onion until soft, add the mushrooms to the pan and cook for a further 2 or 3 minutes.

Add the breadcrumbs, tomato centres, herbs and seasoning, mix well and spoon the stuffing into the tomato shells. Replace the tops.

Place on a greased baking tray and bake for about 10 minutes.

Vegetable casserole

2 servings   *Each serving 5 CHO   330 Cals*

2 large courgettes or slices of   2 large courgettes or slices of
  marrow   marrow

1 small onion   1 small onion

2 medium tomatoes   2 medium tomatoes

½ green pepper, optional   ½ green pepper, optional

1 oz butter or margarine   30 g butter or margarine

2 teaspoons oil   2 teaspoons oil

½ oz flour   15 g flour

7 fl oz stock   200 ml stock

2 oz grated cheese   55 g grated cheese

seasoning   seasoning

Peel and slice the onion and tomatoes. De-seed and slice the pepper.
  Top, tail and slice the courgettes. If marrow is used it should be
  peeled before slicing.

Heat the oil and half the butter in a heavy saucepan and fry the
  courgettes. When soft, remove them from the pan, add the onion
  and fry it.

Add the rest of the vegetables and the seasoning to the pan and simmer
  gently, stirring from time to time until everything is cooked (about
  35 minutes). Return the courgettes to the pan.

Make a sauce with the remaining butter, flour and stock and when the
  sauce is bubbling, stir in half the cheese. (See p. 9.)

Put the vegetables in a shallow fireproof dish, pour on the sauce,
  sprinkle with the rest of the cheese and brown under a hot grill.

Variations: Aubergines, celery, cauliflower or mushrooms may be
  included.

Winter salad

4 servings   *Each serving 5 CHO   28 Cals*

8 oz white cabbage	225 g white cabbage
2 oz carrots	55 g carrots
½ oz raisins	15 g raisins
2 celery sticks	2 celery sticks
gherkins or pickled cucumbers	gherkins or pickled cucumbers
onion rings	onion rings
seasoning	seasoning

Slice the cabbage finely and grate the trimmed carrots.
Trim and dice the celery.
Wash the raisins.
Slice the gherkins and mix them with the raisins and vegetables and
    season to taste.
Garnish with onion rings.

Desserts

If you develop diabetes in middle or later life, the hardest part of treatment may be changing the eating habits of a lifetime. You will probably be told you are overweight and of course it is best if you can lose your 'sweet tooth' as soon as possible. But if you have not reached this happy state and feel a meal is incomplete without a pudding, you will find in this section a few recipes with low Calorie values— within the 50 Calories you have probably been advised is your limit for a dessert.

There are, however, very few ingredients from which low Calorie desserts can be made, so the variety cannot be wide. You may therefore decide to settle for fresh fruit which is lower in Calories than almost any made-up sweet dish.

Fructose and sorbitol are used in some of the recipes and the properties of these products are explained in the Introduction (see pp. 6–7). It is as well to remember that, while these substances are carbohydrate free, both have high Calorie values and should be avoided by slimmers.

Saccharin which has no carbohydrate or Calorie content can be used to sweeten puddings where no bulk is required, and it can be crushed and dissolved in a little water and added to fruit after cooking. In milk puddings it can be added before cooking. If you take one tablet in a cup of tea or coffee, one tablet per serving will probably be sweet enough for you in cooking. If you like two or more in your tea, you can add more saccharin to your sweet course.

Some diabetics have quite high carbohydrate allowances so recipes with up to 25 grams of carbohydrate have been included.

Apple blush

4 servings   *Each serving 15 CHO   116 Cals*

1 lb cooking apples	455 g cooking apples
1 fl oz water	30 ml water
1 tablespoon Ribena	1 tablespoon Ribena
2 fl oz double cream	55 ml double cream
a few drops of vanilla essence	a few drops of vanilla essence

Peel, core and slice the apples and stew them gently in the water for about 15 minutes until soft.

Rub through a sieve and stir in the Ribena.

Chill.

Beat the cream until stiff, add the vanilla essence and spread over the apple.

Apple charlotte

2 servings   *Each serving 15 CHO   108 Cals*

5 oz cooking apple, peeled and cored	140 g cooking apple, peeled and cored
2 teaspoons of sorbitol	2 teaspoons of sorbitol
1 oz soft breadcrumbs	30 g soft breadcrumbs
$\frac{1}{4}$ oz butter or margarine	10 g butter or margarine

Preheat the oven to 375°F/Mark 5.

Stew the apple in a little water and add the sorbitol.

Put alternate layers of apple and breadcrumbs in a small, lightly greased ovenproof dish. Finish with a layer of crumbs.

Dot with butter and bake until the breadcrumbs are lightly browned (30 minutes).

121

Apple and cinnamon slice

6 slices   *Each slice 5 CHO   100 Cals*

3 eggs   3 eggs
2 medium sized cooking apples   2 medium sized cooking apples
crushed saccharin to taste   crushed saccharin to taste
   (3 tablets)   (3 tablets)
8 oz cottage cheese, sieved   225 g cottage cheese, sieved
3 teaspoons of cinnamon   3 teaspoons of cinnamon

Preheat the oven to 350°F/Mark 4.
Separate the eggs and beat the yolks until creamy.
Core, peel and slice the apples very thinly and add the crushed
   saccharin to taste.
Mix the yolks, apples, cottage cheese and cinnamon, blending well.
Beat the egg whites until stiff and fold into the mixture.
Line a 6-in cake tin with lightly oiled greaseproof paper or foil. Fill
   with the mixture and bake for about 30 minutes.
Sprinkle with a little extra cinnamon before serving.

Apple fritters

8 fritters   *Each fritter 10 CHO   80 Cals*

¾ lb cooking apples, trimmed	340 g cooking apples, trimmed
1 oz flour	30 g flour
1 teaspoon of oil	1 teaspoon of oil
2 saccharin tablets	2 saccharin tablets
pinch of salt	pinch of salt
warm water	warm water
1 egg white	1 egg white
1 oz fat for frying	30 g fat for frying
¾ oz castor sugar	20 g castor sugar

Pare and core the apples and slice into eight rings.

Dissolve the saccharin in a little water and soak the rings in it for half an hour.

Sift the flour and salt into a basin, add the oil and two tablespoons of warm water. Stir well and then beat until smooth. Leave to stand for half an hour.

Beat the egg white until stiff and fold into the batter.

Heat the frying fat (preferably a mixture of butter and oil) in a pan.

Spear each apple ring on a fork, dip in the batter and drop immediately into the hot fat.

Fry rather slowly on both sides until crisp and lightly browned. Drain well and keep hot.

Before serving dredge the fritters with the sugar.

Banana custard

2 servings   *Each serving 15 CHO   160 Cals*

1 banana	1 banana
1 beaten egg	1 beaten egg
7 fl oz hot milk	200 ml hot milk
$\frac{1}{4}$ oz diabetic chocolate	10 g diabetic chocolate
1 or 2 saccharin tablets (crushed)	1 or 2 saccharin tablets (crushed)

Put the beaten egg into the top of a double saucepan or in a bowl over a saucepan of hot water.

Add saccharin tablets according to taste.

Pour on the hot, but not boiling, milk and stir until the custard thickens.

Peel and slice the banana into a small serving dish.

Cover the banana slices with the custard and leave to cool.

Decorate with grated chocolate.

Blackberry mousse

4 servings   *Each serving 10 CHO   180 Cals*

8 oz blackberries	225 g blackberries
1 oz castor sugar	30 g castor sugar
1 tablespoon lemon juice	1 tablespoon lemon juice
1 teaspoon gelatine	1 teaspoon gelatine
2 tablespoons of water	2 tablespoons of water
4 fl oz whipping cream	115 ml whipping cream
2 egg whites	2 egg whites

If fresh blackberries are used, wash and drain. Frozen fruit need not be
    thawed before use.

Place the fruit in a saucepan with the lemon juice and sugar and simmer
    gently over a low heat for about 10 minutes until the blackberries
    are soft. Rub through a sieve.

Dissolve the gelatine in the water (see p. 9) and stir into the fruit.

Leave in a cool place until the mousse begins to set.

Whisk the cream and fold in.

Whisk the egg whites until stiff and fold into the mixture.

Chill before serving.

Blackberry & apple pudding (suet)

6 servings   *Each serving 20 CHO   212 Cals*

Crust:

4 oz flour	115 g flour
2 oz suet	55 g suet
½ level teaspoon salt	½ level teaspoon salt
1 tablespoon water	1 tablespoon water

Filling:

8 oz cooking apples	225 g cooking apples
8 oz blackberries	225 g blackberries
2 oz sorbitol	55 g sorbitol

Mix the crust ingredients together to make an elastic dough. Knead
   lightly until smooth.

Put aside a piece of the dough to cover the top of the pudding, roll out
   the rest and line a 1½ pint pudding basin.

Peel, core and slice the apples.

Fill the lined basin with blackberries, apples and sorbitol in alternate
   layers.

Form a lid with the remaining piece of dough, damp the edges of the
   crust in the basin and press the lid on firmly.

Cover with foil and steam for 2 to 2½ hours.

NOTE: *Rhubarb, blackcurrants or gooseberries can be used for the filling
instead of the blackberries and apples.*

Blackberry & apple crumble

2 servings   *Each serving 20 CHO   205 Cals*

4 oz blackberries, fresh or frozen	115 g blackberries, fresh or frozen
4 oz cooking apples, cored and peeled	115 g cooking apples, cored and peeled
1½ oz flour	45 g flour
½ oz margarine	15 g margarine
½ oz sorbitol	15 g sorbitol
saccharin (1 or 2 tablets)	saccharin (1 or 2 tablets)

Preheat the oven to 375°F/Mark 5.

Slice the apples and stew them with the blackberries in just enough water to prevent them from sticking to the pan. About half a cup should do.

When they are just soft but not mushy, remove the pan from the heat and stir in crushed saccharin to taste.

Put the fruit in a small fireproof dish.

Rub the margarine into the flour until it is the consistency of fine breadcrumbs. Mix in the sorbitol.

Sprinkle the crumble evenly over the fruit and bake for 20 to 25 minutes.

Bread and butter pudding

2 servings Each serving 20 CHO   241 Cals

1½ oz thinly cut bread	45 g thinly cut bread
½ oz butter or margarine	15 g butter or margarine
½ oz currants	15 g currants
1 egg	1 egg
7 fl oz warm milk	200 ml warm milk
crushed saccharin (1 or 2 tablets)	crushed saccharin (1 or 2 tablets)
a few drops of vanilla essence, optional	a few drops of vanilla essence, optional

Preheat the oven to 300°F/Mark 2.

Butter the bread and arrange it in a small pie-dish and scatter with currants.

Beat the egg and add the tepid milk, sweetened to taste with the saccharin. Stir in the vanilla.

Pour over the bread and butter and bake for about half an hour or until the custard has set.

Coffee whip

2 servings   Each serving nil CHO   25 Cals

8 fl oz strong unsweetened coffee	225 ml strong unsweetened coffee
2 teaspoons of gelatine	2 teaspoons of gelatine
crushed saccharin (2 tablets)	crushed saccharin (2 tablets)
1 egg white	1 egg white

Dissolve the gelatine in ½ cup of coffee (see p. 9).

Add the remaining coffee and saccharin to taste.

Leave in a cool place until it begins to set.

Whisk the egg white until stiff and fold into the mixture.

Serve chilled.

Diabetic squash jelly

2 servings   *Each serving nil CHO   32 Cals*

4 fl oz lemon, orange or lime diabetic squash	115 ml lemon, orange or lime diabetic squash
1 rounded teaspoon of gelatine	1 rounded teaspoon of gelatine
6 fl oz water	170 ml water

Dissolve the gelatine in the water (see p. 9).
Stir in the diabetic squash, pour into 2 small dishes or 1 larger serving
dish and leave to set.
Serve chilled.

Frothy spiced yoghurt

2 servings   *Each serving 5 CHO   113 Cals*

5 fl oz natural low fat yoghurt	140 ml natural low fat yoghurt
1 egg	1 egg
$\frac{1}{4}$ oz plain diabetic chocolate	10 g plain diabetic chocolate
1 level teaspoon fructose	1 level teaspoon fructose
$\frac{1}{2}$ level teaspoon ground mixed spices or cinnamon	$\frac{1}{2}$ level teaspoon ground mixed spices or cinnamon

Turn the yoghurt into a mixing bowl, stand this over a pan of hot (not
boiling) water over a low heat and stir for 2 or 3 minutes.
Withdraw from the heat.
Separate the egg.
Add the yolk, spices and fructose to the yoghurt and beat well.
Return to the heat and cook for another 3 minutes stirring all the time.
Allow to cool.
Beat the egg white until stiff and fold in with a metal spoon.
Chill.
Before serving sprinkle with grated chocolate.

Fruit juice jelly

2 servings   *Each serving 10 CHO   65 Cals*

8 fl oz unsweetened tinned or
    fresh orange juice
    or
6 fl oz unsweetened tinned
    pineapple juice
1 or 2 saccharin tablets, crushed
¼ oz gelatine
water

225 ml unsweetened tinned or
    fresh orange juice
    or
170 ml unsweetened tinned
    pineapple juice
1 or 2 saccharin tablets, crushed
10 g gelatine
water

Make up the juice to half a pint by adding water.
Dissolve the gelatine in a cup of the liquid (see p. 9) and add the
    crushed saccharin to taste.
Strain the gelatine into the remaining juice and leave in a cool place
    until it begins to set.
Pour into one glass serving dish or two individual glasses.
Leave to set and serve chilled.

Gooseberry fool

4 servings   *Each serving 5 CHO   218 Cals*

1 lb firm gooseberries
1 oz fructose
1 level teaspoon gelatine
5 fl oz thick tinned cream
1 cup of water

455 g firm gooseberries
30 g fructose
1 level teaspoon gelatine
140 ml thick tinned cream
1 cup of water

Wash, top and tail the gooseberries and stew with half a cup of water
    and fructose until soft.
Dissolve the gelatine in the remaining water (see p. 9) and strain into
    the gooseberries.
Allow to cool and reduce to a purée. (See p. 9.)
Fold in the cream and chill before serving.

Gooseberry pie

4 servings   *Each serving 20 CHO   231 Cals*

Pastry:

4 oz flour	115 g flour
1 oz lard	30 g lard
1 oz margarine	30 g margarine
1 tablespoon water	1 tablespoon water
a little milk	a little milk
pinch of salt	pinch of salt

Filling:

1 lb firm gooseberries	455 g firm gooseberries
1 oz fructose	30 g fructose

Preheat the oven to 400°F/Mark 6.

Top and tail the gooseberries, sprinkle with fructose and place them in a piedish.

Make the pastry with the flour, lard, margarine, salt and water (See p. 14.)

Roll it out and cover the fruit.

Prick the pastry and brush it with milk.

Bake for 10 minutes. Reduce the heat to 375°F/Mark 5 and continue cooking for about another 25 minutes.

NOTE: *Forced rhubarb can be used instead of gooseberries.*

Ice cream

2 servings   *Each serving negligible CHO*
                               165 Cals

$3\frac{1}{2}$ fl oz milk   100 ml milk
2 fl oz double cream   55 ml double cream
2 level teaspoons gelatine   2 level teaspoons gelatine
1 level teaspoon fructose   1 level teaspoon fructose
3 tablespoons water   3 tablespoons water
Vanilla, lemon, raspberry or   Vanilla, lemon, raspberry or
    other essence   other essence

Dissolve the gelatine in the water (see p. 9). Stir in the fructose and
    leave to cool but not to set.
Mix together the milk, cream and a few drops of the chosen flavouring
    and stir into the gelatine mixture.
Pour into a freezing tray, turn up the refrigerator to maximum
    strength, and leave for about half an hour. In hot weather a little
    extra time may be necessary.
Stir once or twice during the freezing period.

NOTE : *If raspberry essence is used a little cochineal may be added to
enhance the colour.*

Lemon meringue pie

6 servings   *Each serving 15 CHO   176 Cals*

Pastry:

3 oz flour	85 g flour
$\frac{3}{4}$ oz lard	20 g lard
$\frac{3}{4}$ oz margarine	20 g margarine
1 tablespoon water	1 tablespoon water

Filling:

juice and grated rind of 2 lemons	juice and grated rind of 2 lemons
2 eggs	2 eggs
$\frac{3}{4}$ oz cornflour	20 g cornflour
2 oz sorbitol	55 g sorbitol
5 fl oz water	140 ml water

Preheat the oven to 325°F/Mark 3.

Make the pastry in the usual way (see p. 14), roll it out and line a 7-in flan tin.

Bake blind for 15 minutes (see p. 8).

Mix together the cornflour, lemon juice, water and lemon rind.

Bring the mixture slowly to the boil, stirring all the time.

Withdraw from the heat, stir in the sorbitol and allow to cool slightly.

Separate the eggs, beat in the yolks and pour the mixture into the pastry case.

Whip the egg whites until stiff and spread over the flan.

Bake for 10 to 15 minutes.

Lemon milk jelly

4 servings   *Each serving 5 CHO   75 Cals*

1 large lemon	1 large lemon
14 fl oz milk	400 ml milk
6 fl oz water	170 ml water
½ oz gelatine	15 g gelatine
crushed saccharin (3 tablets)	crushed saccharin (3 tablets)

Wash the lemon and peel it thinly with a sharp knife, taking care not to
   include any of the white pith.

Squeeze out the juice.

Put the rind in a saucepan with a ¼ pint of the water, bring to the boil
   and simmer gently for about 5 minutes.

Add the lemon juice and strain into a mixing bowl. You should have a
   good ¼ pint of liquid.

Dissolve the gelatine in the remaining water (see p. 9) and stir in the
   lemon juice and water.

Add the crushed saccharin and cool slightly before whisking in the cold
   milk.

Pour into a pint mould and leave in a cool place to set.

Turn out and serve.

Lime trifle

2 servings   *Each serving 15 CHO   450 Cals*

1½ oz sponge (2 trifle
    sponge cakes)

1 oz diabetic jam

2 rounded teaspoons gelatine

7 fl oz water

3 fl oz diabetic lime squash
    (undiluted)

4 fl oz whipping cream

nuts or grated diabetic chocolate
    to decorate

45 g sponge (2 trifle
    sponge cakes)

30 g diabetic jam

2 rounded teaspoons gelatine

200 ml water

85 ml diabetic lime squash
    (undiluted)

115 ml whipping cream

nuts or grated diabetic chocolate
    to decorate

Slice the sponge cakes in half and spread with the jam. Sandwich the
    halves together and then cut in slices and line the base of a serving
    dish.

Dissolve the gelatine in the water (see p. 9), add the squash and stir
    well.

Pour the squash mixture over the sponge cakes and leave in a cool
    place to set.

Whip the cream until stiff and spread over the trifle.

Decorate with a few chopped nuts or a little grated diabetic chocolate.

NOTE: *Orange or lemon squash may be used.*

Lemon cheese soufflé

2 servings

Each serving negligible CHO
240 Cals

5 oz cottage cheese	140 g cottage cheese
2 eggs	2 eggs
1 lemon	1 lemon
2 teaspoons fructose	2 teaspoons fructose

Preheat the oven to 400°F/Mark 6.

Grate the lemon rind and squeeze and strain the juice.

Sieve the cottage cheese.

Separate the eggs and beat the yolks with the fructose, cottage cheese, lemon juice and rind.

Beat the whites until stiff and fold into the cheese mixture.

Bake for about 25 minutes in a small greased soufflé dish standing in a pan of water.

Milk puddings

2 servings

Each serving 20 CHO   193 Cals

1 oz rice, tapioca, semolina, sago or macaroni	30 g rice, tapioca, semolina, sago or macaroni
15 fl oz milk	425 ml milk
crushed saccharin (3 or 4 tablets)	crushed saccharin (3 or 4 tablets)
grated nutmeg, optional	grated nutmeg, optional

Place the cereal in a lightly buttered fireproof dish and add the milk.

Preheat the oven to 325°F/Mark 3.

Add the crushed saccharin to taste, stir well and bake for about 15 minutes.

Remove from the oven, stir and return to the oven for about a further hour's cooking or longer if a thicker consistency is preferred.

Sprinkle, if liked, with grated nutmeg before serving.

Mocha chocolate mousse

2 servings   *Each serving negligible CHO*
                                148 Cals

1½ oz plain diabetic chocolate	45 g plain diabetic chocolate
2 eggs	2 eggs
1½ fl oz water	45 ml water
1 level teaspoon instant coffee powder	1 level teaspoon instant coffee powder
1 teaspoon gelatine	1 teaspoon gelatine
1 rounded teaspoon of fructose	1 rounded teaspoon of fructose

Break the chocolate into small pieces in a bowl.
Dissolve the gelatine in the water. (See p. 9.) Add the coffee powder and pour over the chocolate.
Place the bowl over a pan of hot (not boiling) water and stir until the chocolate has melted.
Mix in the fructose.
Remove from the heat and allow to cool but not to set.
Separate the eggs and beat the yolks into the mixture.
Whisk the whites until stiff and fold in.
Serve chilled.

Orange cheesecake

6 servings   ***Each serving 10 CHO   180 Cals***

8 oz cottage cheese	225 g cottage cheese
8 oz low fat natural yoghurt	225 g low fat natural yoghurt
1 small lemon	1 small lemon
1 orange plus 6 orange segments	1 orange plus 6 orange segments
½ oz gelatine	15 g gelatine
1 oz fructose	30 g fructose
or	or
2 oz sorbitol	55 g sorbitol
1 egg white	1 egg white
6 small digestive biscuits	6 small digestive biscuits
2 oz melted butter/margarine	55 g melted butter/margarine

Crush the digestive biscuits and add the melted butter. Mix to a stiff paste.

Grease a shallow 7-in serving dish with butter.

Line the dish with the biscuit mixture.

Sieve the cottage cheese and blend with yoghurt.

Grate the lemon and orange rinds and squeeze the juice from the fruit. Stir into the cheese mixture.

Dissolve the gelatine in 3 tablespoons water (see p. 9). Strain into the mixture. Stir in the fructose or sorbitol.

Whisk the egg white until stiff and fold into the mixture.

Pour onto the biscuit base and leave in a cool place to set.

Decorate with orange segments.

NOTE: *The filling can be made without a biscuit base. The carbohydrate per serving will then be negligible.*

Pineapple mousse

4 servings   *Each serving 10 CHO   188 Cals*

9 fl oz unsweetened pineapple juice	255 ml unsweetened pineapple juice
7 fl oz milk	200 ml milk
1 large egg	1 large egg
2 fl oz water	55 ml water
2 fl oz whipping cream	55 ml whipping cream
2 teaspoons gelatine	2 teaspoons gelatine
½ oz flaked almonds	15 g flaked almonds

Dissolve the gelatine in the water. (See p. 9.)

Separate the egg and put the beaten yolk with the milk in a mixing bowl. Stand this over a pan of hot water. Stir over a low heat until the custard thickens, but do not let it boil.

Pour the custard, gelatine and pineapple juice into a bowl and leave in a cool place, stirring occasionally.

When the mixture is cool and nearly set, whisk the egg white until stiff and fold it in.

Pour into a serving dish and chill.

Whisk the cream and decorate the mousse with this and a few flaked almonds.

Plum & apple meringue

2 servings   *Each serving 10 CHO   47 Cals*

6 oz stewed plums	170 g stewed plums
2½ oz stewed apple	70 g stewed apple
¼ oz semolina	10 g semolina
1 egg white	1 egg white
crushed saccharin (2 or 3 tablets)	crushed saccharin (2 or 3 tablets)
a few flaked almonds, optional	a few flaked almonds, optional

Preheat the oven to 325°F/Mark 3.

Remove the stones from the plums. Sieve the fruit.

Put the fruit purée in a saucepan with the semolina and cook until the mixture thickens, stirring all the time (about 3 minutes).

Remove from the heat and mix in the saccharin.

Allow to cool and then put the mixture in a greased fireproof dish and level with a knife.

Beat the egg white until stiff and spread over the fruit.

Sprinkle with flaked almonds.

Bake for about 20 minutes until the meringue is lightly browned.

Serve hot or cold.

Queen of puddings

1 serving   *20 CHO   253 Cals*

1 egg	1 egg
3 fl oz milk	85 ml milk
1 lemon	1 lemon
1 oz soft breadcrumbs	30 g soft breadcrumbs
1 crushed saccharin tablet	1 crushed saccharin tablet
1 teaspoon diabetic jam	1 teaspoon diabetic jam

Preheat the oven to 325°F/Mark 3.
Separate the egg.
Grate the rind and squeeze the juice from the lemon.
Warm the milk, dissolve the saccharin in it and beat in the yolk.
Put the breadcrumbs in a small ovenproof dish, pour on the yolk and
    milk mixture. Add the rind and juice of the lemon and stir in.
Bake until the pudding is set (20 to 30 minutes). Then remove from the
    oven and spread with jam.
Whisk the egg white until stiff and pile on the top.
Return to the oven and bake for a further 10 minutes.

Rhubarb sponge

4 servings   *Each serving 10 CHO   202 Cals*

1 lb rhubarb	455 g rhubarb
2 oz self-raising flour	55 g self-raising flour
1 oz margarine	30 g margarine
1½ oz fructose	45 g fructose
2 eggs	2 eggs
water	water

Preheat the oven to 350°F/Mark 4.

Trim and cut the rhubarb into short lengths and stew in a little water until soft but not pulpy.

Stir in half the fructose.

Cream the margarine with the remaining fructose, sift in the flour and add the beaten egg. Beat well.

Grease a deep pie dish, pour in the rhubarb and top with the sponge mixture.

Bake for about 25 minutes or until the sponge has risen and is golden brown.

Soufflé omelette

1 serving   *Negligible CHO   366 Cals*

2 eggs	2 eggs
1 teaspoon fructose	1 teaspoon fructose
½ oz oil or butter	15 g oil or butter
1 teaspoon diabetic jam	1 teaspoon diabetic jam
1 tablespoon water	1 tablespoon water

Separate the eggs and whisk the yolks with the water and fructose until
    they are pale and creamy
Whisk the whites until stiff and fold into the yolk mixture.
Heat the fat in an omelette pan, pour in the mixture and level off with a
    palette knife.
Cook without moving the contents of the pan until the bottom of the
    omelette is set and a pale golden brown.
Set the top under a hot grill for about half a minute.
Spread the omelette with warmed diabetic jam, fold over and slide onto
    a warmed plate.
Serve immediately.

Summer pudding

4 servings   *Each serving 20 CHO   107 Cals*

4 oz thinly sliced bread, without crusts	115 g thinly sliced bread, without crusts
$\frac{3}{4}$ lb blackberries	340 g blackberries
$\frac{1}{2}$ oz fructose	15 g fructose
4 fl oz water	115 ml water

Line a small pudding basin with all the bread except one slice.

Stew the blackberries in the water with the fructose for about 5 minutes. The berries should be moist but not floating in the juice.

Pour off and save any surplus liquid.

Fill the lined bowl with the fruit and cover with the remaining bread. Put a plate or piece of foil on top and press well down.

Leave in a cool place, with a weight on top, for several hours.

Turn out and use the remaining juice to cover any small uncoloured patches of bread.

NOTE: *A mixture of berries may be used providing some are strongly coloured enough to stain the bread.*

Vanilla whip

2 servings   *Each serving 5 CHO   155 Cals*

---

1 egg	1 egg
½ oz fructose	15 g fructose
7 fl oz milk	200 ml milk
1 level teaspoon gelatine	1 level teaspoon gelatine
vanilla essence	vanilla essence
1 tablespoon water	1 tablespoon water

Separate the egg and beat the yolk with the fructose until creamy.

Add about 5 drops of vanilla essence to the milk and stir into the yolk.

Dissolve the gelatine in the water (see p. 9) and strain it into the milk and egg mixture.

Heat the mixture in a double saucepan, or in a bowl standing over a pan of hot but not boiling water, and stir until the custard thickens.

Remove from the heat and leave to cool but not to set.

Whisk the egg white until stiff and fold into the mixture.

Serve well chilled.

Bakery

If you are on a reducing diet, you should ignore this section. It is not possible to make cakes, buns or biscuits without flour and fat. The use of sorbitol or fructose instead of sugar reduces the carbohydrate but not the Calories.

Although sorbitol provides bulk, it lacks the ability of sugar to make sponge cakes rise. In some recipes, therefore, a mixture of sugar and sorbitol is used and this gives cakes a good texture and flavour, though they will be a little drier than they would be if made with sugar only.

146

An important point to remember when baking with sorbitol is that it requires more beating than sugar. Five minutes is the minimum time recommended.

You could try adapting your own non-diabetic recipes merely by substituting sorbitol for sugar. Instructions on how this can be done are given in the Introduction. (See pp. 10–12.)

Fructose is twice as sweet as sugar and when used in its place only half the quantity will be needed.

Both fructose and sorbitol are satisfactory in biscuit making.

When using yeast, a few points are worth bearing in mind. A warm, steamy, draught-free atmosphere and warm ingredients and kitchen utensils make yeast work more quickly. Yeast needs sugar to make it work. Salt slows its action so always mix the salt in with the flour and never with the yeast.

Fresh yeast is not always easy to obtain but dried yeast is a good substitute. You will want about half the quantity of dried yeast to fresh, and you should mix it with one part boiling water to two parts cold. Just stir the yeast and water together and let it stand in a warm place. A frothy head should appear on the mixture in 10 to 15 minutes. If the yeast does not froth, this could mean it is stale. Fresh yeast will keep in a screw-top jar in the refrigerator for more than a week. If dried yeast is stored in a cool, dry place it should keep its active life for up to 6 months.

Bread making is a satisfying business but it is time-consuming and it is therefore best to make fairly large quantities. Three loaves are as easy to make as one, and in fact bigger quantities of dough are easier to handle. Home-made bread will keep in a refrigerator for up to a fortnight and for much longer in a deep freeze, but it should be baked before putting into cold storage. Freezing interferes with the action of the yeast so raw dough should not be stored.

Banana bread

15 slices   *Each slice 20 CHO   194 Cals*

4 oz margarine	115 g margarine
4 oz brown sugar	115 g brown sugar
4 oz sorbitol	115 g sorbitol
1 egg	1 egg
2 ripe bananas	2 ripe bananas
8 oz plain flour	225 g plain flour
1½ teaspoons baking powder	1½ teaspoons baking powder
1 teaspoon salt	1 teaspoon salt
5 oz natural low-fat yoghurt (one carton)	140 g natural low-fat yoghurt (one carton)

Preheat oven to 350°F/Mark 4.

Beat the margarine, sugar and sorbitol together for 5 minutes.

Beat in the egg.

Mash the bananas and combine these with the mixture.

Sift the flour, baking powder and salt and add half to the banana mixture with half the yoghurt. Mix well.

Add the remaining flour and yoghurt and mix again.

Place the mixture in a greased loaf tin [8 in × 4 in] and bake for an hour in the middle of the oven.

Turn out and allow to cool on a wire rack.

Bread

Wheatmeal bread

1 large loaf or 2 small loaves $\frac{2}{3}$ *oz = 10 grams CHO*   *46 Cals*

8 oz strong white bread flour	225 g strong white bread flour
8 oz wholemeal flour	225 g wholemeal flour
¼ oz lard or 1 tablespoon oil	10 g lard or 1 tablespoon oil
½ pint water	285 ml water
2 level teaspoons of dried yeast	2 level teaspoons of dried yeast
1 level teaspoon of sugar	1 level teaspoon of sugar
¼ oz salt	10 g salt

White bread

3 large loaves $\frac{2}{3}$ *oz = 10 grams CHO*   *46 Cals*

3 lb plain white flour	1 kilo 350 g plain white flour
1 oz lard	30 g lard
1 oz dried yeast	30 g dried yeast
1 teaspoon of sugar	1 teaspoon of sugar
½ oz salt	15 g salt
1½ pints water	850 ml water

Method (suitable for both white and brown bread)

Sift the flour and salt into a large mixing bowl. If the ingredients are very cold stand the bowl in a warm place for a few minutes. Rub in the lard, or stir in the oil.

Bring one-third of the water to the boil and add to the remaining two-thirds of cold water. Take ¼ pint of this tepid water and whisk into it the dried yeast and the sugar. Leave for 10–15 minutes until frothy and then mix with the remaining water.

Add the yeast mixture to the flour to form a dough. Knead for 10 minutes on a floured surface. Leave the dough in the bowl to prove. The bowl should be covered with a damp tea-towel and the proving will take about an hour in a warm room. When proving has finished the dough should have doubled its original size.

Preheat the oven to 450°F/Mark 8.

Remove the dough from the bowl and knead it for 1 minute. Divide it into three pieces and put each into a large loaf tin (a 2-lb tin). The wholemeal bread will only make sufficient dough for one large or two small tins.

Leave the dough to rise for a second time. If left in a warm room for an hour the dough should rise to the top of the tin.

Bake for 20 to 30 minutes depending on the size of the loaf. Turn out. If the bottoms of the loaves are spongy, return the loaves to the oven upside down for a few minutes.

NOTE: *After the first kneading, the wholemeal dough can be put into the loaf tins. These should be half-filled and the bread can be baked as soon as the dough has risen to the top of the tins.*

Butterfly cakes

10 cakes   *Each cake 10 CHO   120 Cals*

1 oz castor sugar	30 g castor sugar
1 oz sorbitol	30 g sorbitol
2 oz margarine	55 g margarine
3 oz self-raising flour	85 g self-raising flour
$\frac{1}{4}$ teaspoon baking powder	$\frac{1}{4}$ teaspoon baking powder
1 egg	1 egg
2 teaspoons milk	2 teaspoons milk
vanilla essence	vanilla essence
$1\frac{1}{2}$ fl oz whipping cream	45 ml whipping cream

Preheat the oven to 375°F/Mark 5.

Cream together the sugar, sorbitol and margarine.

Blend in the flour, baking powder, beaten egg, milk and about a quarter of a teaspoon of vanilla essence.

Beat very thoroughly by hand or with an electric beater.

Grease generously 10 bun tins and put about a dessertspoon of the mixture in each.

Bake in the top half of the oven for about 20 minutes. Turn out of the tins and leave to cool on a rack.

Whip the cream with a few drops of vanilla essence until stiff.

Cut a circle from the top of each cake, put a small blob of cream on the cake and arrange the cut-out piece of sponge in two wings.

Chelsea buns

12 buns   *Each bun 20 CHO 157 Cals*

3 fl oz water	85 ml water
1 level teaspoon sugar	1 level teaspoon sugar
1 level teaspoon dried yeast	1 level teaspoon dried yeast
8 oz plain flour	225 g plain flour
1 egg	1 egg
pinch of salt	pinch of salt
2 oz margarine	55 g margarine
$\frac{3}{4}$ oz sorbitol	20 g sorbitol
2 fl oz milk	55 ml milk
1 oz margarine (melted)	30 g margarine (melted)
1 oz currants	30 g currants
1 oz sultanas	30 g sultanas
1 oz candied peel	30 g candied peel

Preheat oven to 400°F/Mark 6.

Heat the water to a temperature at which you can just bear to dip in a
 finger and pour it into a small bowl.

Add the sugar, sprinkle on the yeast and whisk well. Leave in a warm
 place until a good frothy head forms. This should take 10–15
 minutes.

Sieve the warmed flour into a warmed mixing bowl, make a well in the
 middle and pour in the yeast liquid.

Add the beaten egg, salt, the unmelted margarine, milk and sorbitol.

Knead well on a floured board to form a soft, slack dough which is
 smooth and does not stick to the hands.

Return to the bowl, cover with a damp cloth and leave in a warm place
 until the dough has doubled in size.

Roll out into a square about 12 in by 12 in, brush with melted
 margarine and sprinkle with dried fruit.

Roll up the dough like a swiss roll and cut into twelve 1-in slices.

Place on a greased baking tray with sides, cover and leave in a warm
 place to prove again until each bun has risen to about $1\frac{1}{2}$ in high.

Bake for 15 to 20 minutes in the middle of the oven.

Chocolate biscuits

20 biscuits   *2 biscuits 5 CHO   96 Cals*

2½ oz flour	70 g flour
2 oz margarine	55 g margarine
2 oz ground almonds	55 g ground almonds
2 oz sorbitol	55 g sorbitol
½ oz cocoa powder	15 g cocoa powder
1 egg	1 egg
pinch of salt	pinch of salt

Preheat the oven to 325°F/Mark 3.
Beat the margarine and sorbitol together until fluffy.
Stir in the beaten egg.
Sift the flour, cocoa, almonds and salt into the mixture and beat until
    well mixed.
Grease a baking sheet and place 20 teaspoons of the mixture on it.
Flatten to form a biscuit shape and bake for 15 to 20 minutes on the
    middle shelf of the oven.

Chocolate cake

12 slices   *Each slice 20 CHO   258 Cals*

5 oz self-raising flour	140 g self-raising flour
1 oz cocoa powder	30 g cocoa powder
6 oz soft margarine	170 g soft margarine
3 eggs	3 eggs
3 oz castor sugar	85 g castor sugar
3 oz sorbitol	85 g sorbitol
$1\frac{1}{2}$ oz (1 tablespoon) golden syrup	45 g (1 tablespoon) golden syrup
1 fl oz milk	30 ml milk

Preheat the oven to 350°F/Mark 4.

Beat together the margarine, sugar and sorbitol until fluffy and then beat in the eggs, syrup and milk.

Sift in the flour and cocoa and beat for 5 minutes.

Grease a 7-in cake tin, fill with the mixture and bake for $1\frac{1}{4}$ hours.

Chocolate éclairs

10 éclairs   *Each éclair 5 CHO   215 Cals*

1½ oz butter	45 g butter
5 fl oz water	140 ml water
2½ oz flour	70 g flour
3 eggs	3 eggs
5 fl oz whipping cream	140 ml whipping cream
a few drops vanilla essence	a few drops vanilla essence
6 oz diabetic chocolate	170 g diabetic chocolate
5 fl oz hot water	140 ml hot water

Preheat the oven to 425°F/Mark 7.

Melt the butter in a saucepan, add the water, bring to the boil and then remove from the heat.

Add the sifted flour quickly and stir vigorously over a low heat until the mixture forms a ball which leaves the side of the pan. Remove from the heat.

Beat in the eggs one by one until the mixture is soft.

Pipe ten éclair cases onto a greased baking tray and bake for about 30 minutes.

When the éclairs are well-risen and golden, remove them from the oven, slit each to let out the steam.

Leave to cool on a rack.

Whip the cream until stiff, fold in the vanilla essence and sorbitol and fill the éclair cases.

Mix the melted diabetic chocolate with ¼ pint hot water. Coat the éclair cases with the chocolate icing.

Coffee sponge

½ oz sugar	15 g sugar
2 oz fructose	55 g fructose
2 oz margarine	55 g margarine
1 large egg	1 large egg
2½ oz self-raising flour	70 g self-raising flour
2 rounded teaspoons instant coffee	2 rounded teaspoons instant coffee
1 tablespoon water, heated	1 tablespoon water, heated

Preheat the oven to 375°F/Mark 5.

Cream together the sugar, fructose and margarine and beat well for about 5 minutes.

Whisk the egg then gradually beat it into the mixture.

Fold in the sifted flour.

Dissolve the coffee in the hot water and mix in well.

Grease a 6-in cake tin, fill with the mixture and bake for about 15 minutes.

Turn out and leave to cool on a wire rack.

Date & spice cake

12 slices   *Each slice 15 CHO   122 Cals*

5 oz self-raising flour	140 g self-raising flour
2 oz sorbitol	55 g sorbitol
2 oz margarine	55 g margarine
4 oz dates, stoned	115 g dates, stoned
3 fl oz water	85 ml water
level teaspoon mixed spice	level teaspoon mixed spice
level teaspoon bicarbonate of soda	level teaspoon bicarbonate of soda
1 fl oz milk	30 ml milk

Preheat the oven to 350°F/Mark 4.
Chop the dates and stew them in the water for 5 minutes.
Sieve the flour, sorbitol, spice and bicarbonate of soda and rub in the fat.
Add the dates and the water in which they have cooked as well as the milk to the flour mixture and beat for 5 minutes.
Grease a 6-in cake tin and fill with the mixture.
Bake on the middle shelf of the oven for 35 minutes.

Drop scones

10 scones   *Each scone 5 CHO   50 Cals*

2½ oz plain flour	70 g plain flour
pinch of salt	pinch of salt
½ teaspoon fructose	½ teaspoon fructose
1 small egg	1 small egg
½ oz melted butter	15 g melted butter
2½ fl oz milk	70 ml milk

Preheat a girdle or heavy frying pan over a moderate heat.

Sift all the dry ingredients into a mixing bowl, make a well in the centre and drop in the egg and melted butter.

Add the milk gradually and beat well with a wooden spoon.

Grease the girdle or pan very lightly and pour the mixture from a jug or the point of a spoon to make neat circles.

As soon as the scones are puffed and bubbling and the undersides lightly browned, turn them with a palette knife and brown the other side.

Serve immediately or place between the folds of a clean, warmed teatowel until required.

Fruit cake

12 slices   *Each slice 15 CHO   160 Cals*

6 oz self-raising flour	170 g self-raising flour
2 oz margarine	55 g margarine
4 oz sorbitol	115 g sorbitol
4 oz mixed dried fruit	115 g mixed dried fruit
5 fl oz milk	140 ml milk
1 teaspoon bicarbonate of soda	1 teaspoon bicarbonate of soda
2 teaspoons vinegar	2 teaspoons vinegar
5 or 6 drops orange or lemon essence	5 or 6 drops orange or lemon essence

Preheat the oven to 325°F/Mark 3.

Sift the flour and bicarbonate of soda into a bowl and rub in the margarine.

Add the sorbitol and dried fruit and mix well.

Stir in the milk and essence, add the vinegar and beat for at least 5 minutes.

Grease a round 6-in cake tin, fill with the mixture and bake for 1 hour.

Ginger fairlings

10 biscuits   *Each biscuit 10 CHO   87 Cals*

$1\frac{1}{2}$ oz butter or margarine	45 g butter or margarine
$\frac{3}{4}$ oz golden syrup (2 teaspoons)	20 g golden syrup (2 teaspoons)
3 oz self-raising flour	85 g self-raising flour
a pinch of bicarbonate of soda	a pinch of bicarbonate of soda
1 teaspoon dried ginger	1 teaspoon dried ginger
$1\frac{1}{2}$ oz sorbitol	45 g sorbitol

Preheat the oven to 375°F/Mark 5.

Melt the butter and syrup in a saucepan over a low heat.

Sift the flour, bicarbonate of soda, sorbitol and ginger into the melted butter and syrup and mix well together.

Using a teaspoon, form into 10 balls and place on an ungreased baking sheet, flatten slightly and leave plenty of room for spreading.

Bake for 10 to 15 minutes in the middle of the oven.

Golden oatmeal biscuits

28 Biscuits   *Each biscuit 5 CHO   56 Cals*

3 oz self-raising flour   85 g self-raising flour
2 oz sorbitol   55 g sorbitol
2 oz oatmeal   55 g oatmeal
2 teaspoons golden syrup   2 teaspoons golden syrup
1½ oz lard   45 g lard
2 oz margarine   55 g margarine
1 level teaspoon baking powder   1 level teaspoon baking powder

Preheat the oven to 350° F/ Mark 4.

Melt the fats and syrup in a bowl over hot water then add all the dry
   ingredients and mix well together.
Using a teaspoon, form into 28 balls and place these on a baking sheet
   leaving room for spreading.
Bake for about 15 minutes on the middle shelf of the oven.
The biscuits should still be soft when taken from the oven and should be
   left on the trays for a few minutes before being transferred to a rack
   to cool.

Jam tartlets

12 tartlets   *Each tartlet 10 CHO   142 Cals*

6 oz plain flour	170 g plain flour
1½ oz lard	45 g lard
1½ oz margarine	45 g margarine
1 tablespoon water	1 tablespoon water
diabetic jam	diabetic jam

Preheat the oven to 375°F/Mark 5.

Make the pastry with the flour, lard, margarine and water and roll it out.

Lightly grease 12 patty tins, line with the pastry and prick the bases with a fork. Put a teaspoonful of diabetic jam in each case.

Bake in the middle of the oven for about 15 minutes.

Remove from the tins and cool on a rack.

Madeleines

8 cakes   *Each cake 5 CHO   147 Cals*

2 oz self-raising flour	55 g self-raising flour
2 oz sorbitol	55 g sorbitol
1 egg	1 egg
2 oz soft margarine	55 g soft margarine
2 teaspoons diabetic jam	2 teaspoons diabetic jam
1 oz desiccated coconut	30 g desiccated coconut

Preheat the oven to 350°F/Mark 4.

Whisk the egg.

Sieve the flour and sorbitol into a bowl and mix together.

Add the egg and beat well.

Add the margarine and beat the mixture again very thoroughly.

Put into 8 lightly greased madeleine cases or small patty tins and bake for about 15 minutes.

Spread thinly with diabetic jam, diluted if necessary with a little cold water, and roll the madeleines in the coconut.

Scones

6 scones   *Each scone 15 CHO   131 Cals*

4 oz self-raising flour	115 g self-raising flour
1½ oz margarine	45 g margarine
1 level teaspoon cream of tartar	1 level teaspoon cream of tartar
½ level teaspoon baking powder	½ level teaspoon baking powder
2½ fl oz milk	70 ml milk
pinch of salt	pinch of salt

Preheat the oven to 400°F/Mark 6.

Sift the flour, cream of tartar, baking powder and salt into a bowl and rub in the margarine.

Add the milk and work to form a stiff dough.

Using floured hands, form the dough into a sausage shape about 2 in across, flatten the ends and cut into six equal rounds.

Place the rounds on a floured baking sheet, brush the tops with milk and bake for about 15 to 20 minutes.

Variations:

Currant Scones

Add 1½ oz (45 g) currants to the basic mixture before adding the milk. The CHO value of each scone will be 20 and 148 Cals.

Cheese Scones

Add 1 oz (30 g) grated Cheddar cheese to the basic mixture before adding the milk. This will increase the Calorie value of each scone to 151 Calories.

Shortbread

12 biscuits   *Each biscuit 10 CHO   144 Cals*

6 oz flour	170 g flour
4 oz butter or margarine	115 g butter or margarine
2 oz fructose	55 g fructose

Preheat the oven to 350°F/Mark 4.

Rub the fat into the flour, mix in the fructose and work the mixture well until a stiff dough is formed.

Roll out on a lightly floured board, cut into 12 fingers of equal size and prick with a fork.

Bake for 15 to 20 minutes on a lightly greased baking tray in the middle of the oven.

Sweet oatmeal fingers

12 fingers   *Each finger 10 CHO   140 Cals*

4 oz margarine (not soft)	115 g margarine (not soft)
1½ oz Demerara sugar	45 g Demerara sugar
1½ oz sorbitol	45 g sorbitol
4 oz porridge oats	115 g porridge oats

Preheat the oven to 375°F/Mark 5.

Melt the margarine in a mixing bowl over a pan of hot water.

Put the sugar, sorbitol and oats in another bowl, mix well, and add these ingredients to the melted margarine.

Stir until thoroughly blended.

Grease well a baking tray about 7 in by 11 in, press the mixture into this and level off with a palette knife.

Bake for 15 to 20 minutes.

While still hot in the tray, cut into 12 fingers.

Allow to cool completely before removing from the tray.

Victoria sponge

8 slices   *Each slice 20 CHO   247 Cals*

4 oz margarine (soft)   115 g margarine (soft)

2 oz castor sugar   55 g castor sugar

2 oz fructose   55 g fructose

4 oz self-raising flour   115 g self-raising flour

1 level teaspoon baking powder   1 level teaspoon baking powder

2 large eggs   2 large eggs

3 or 4 drops vanilla or lemon   3 or 4 drops vanilla or lemon
   essence   essence

2 teaspoons diabetic jam or   2 teaspoons diabetic jam or
   lemon curd   lemon curd

Preheat the oven to 350°F/Mark 3.

Beat the margarine, sugar and fructose until smooth. Add the beaten eggs gradually.

Fold in the sifted flour and baking powder and vanilla essence (vanilla if jam is to be used and lemon for a lemon curd filling).

Beat for at least 2 minutes.

Grease two 7-in sandwich tins, line the bases with greaseproof paper and divide the mixture into tins. Level off with a palette knife.

Bake in the middle of the oven for about 30 minutes.

Turn out onto a wire rack and when cold, sandwich the halves together with diabetic jam or lemon curd.

Chocolate icing

Total: 30 CHO   2160 Cals

4 oz plain diabetic chocolate	115 g plain diabetic chocolate
3 fl oz hot water	85 ml hot water

Break up the chocolate and put the pieces in a mixing bowl over a pan
   of hot, but not boiling water and stir until the chocolate melts.
Remove from the heat and beat in the hot water.
Spread over the cake immediately with a palette knife dipped in hot
   water.

White icing

Nil CHO   400 Cals

3½ oz sorbitol powder	100 g sorbitol powder
vanilla essence to taste	vanilla essence to taste
6 teaspoons lemon juice	6 teaspoons lemon juice
about 18 drops water	about 18 drops water

Care should be taken in adding liquid to the sorbitol. After each drop
   of liquid is added, the mixture should be well beaten to ensure that
   the moisture is evenly distributed throughout the sorbitol.
Spread over the cake with a palette knife which has been warmed in hot
   water.

Cream & fruit sandwich filling

Total 10 CHO   2160 Cals

4 fl oz whipping cream
4 oz strawberries, raspberries,
    peaches or cherries

115 ml whipping cream
115 g strawberries, raspberries,
    peaches or cherries

If strawberries or peaches are used, cut the fruit into slices.
Remove the stones from the cherries.
Whip the cream until stiff and spread on the bottom half of a sponge
    cake.
Spread the fruit on the cream and sandwich the cake together with the
    other half.
The carbohydrate value per slice of the filling will be negligible.

Nut & banana sandwich filling

Total 10 CHO   419 Cals

1 banana
2 oz blanched nuts
1 fl oz whipping cream
2 teaspoons lemon juice

1 banana
55 g blanched nuts
30 ml whipping cream
2 teaspoons lemon juice

Mash the banana with the lemon juice.
Chop and mix in the nuts and bind with the cream.
Spread the bottom half of a sponge cake with the filling and sandwich
    the cake together with the other half.
The carbohydrate value per slice of the filling will be negligible.

166

Preserves and pickles

Making jams and marmalades with sorbitol and fructose is as easy as making normal preserves and the same basic principles apply, but it is necessary to know the properties of these two products and how they differ from sugar. It should then be a simple matter to adapt your own recipes. Chemists do not always have these artificial sweeteners in stock so it may be necessary to order them in advance.

Preserves made with sorbitol and fructose have the same calorie value as those containing sugar and they are not therefore suitable for anyone who needs to lose weight. Sorbitol contains no carbohydrate: fructose (fruit sugar) is a carbohydrate but in the main does not require insulin to convert it into energy for the body's needs. It is twice as sweet as sugar so less of it need be used.

A teaspoonful of jam or marmalade made with sorbitol or fructose can be reckoned as giving between 1 and 2 grams of carbohydrate (CHO) according to the fruit used, and can be regarded as negligible in the diet. Only one person in the household will probably be using jams or marmalades made with artificial sweeteners. It is therefore recommended that small quantities be made anyway to start with, that small containers are used and that these should be stored in a cool place. These preserves can harden after a time and occasionally, when sorbitol is used, white patches can appear which look like mould but are hard and crystalline. In either event, empty the contents of the pots into a pan, add 2 fl oz of water to every pound of jam, bring to the boil and simmer for about five minutes. Repot in clean warm jars and use as soon as possible. All fruits should be in good condition, washed and drained, with hulls and stalks removed. Soft fruit should be heated in the pan with a minimum of water until the juice runs out. Harder fruits like plums need rather more water — about half a pint to every 2 to 3 lb fruit.

Apples, plums, blackcurrants, redcurrants, raspberries, gooseberries and blackberries contain a lot of pectin and need no extra setting agent. Strawberries and cherries have little natural pectin. One tablespoon of lemon juice added to every 1 lb (455 g) of fruit can aid setting and counteract the excessive sweetness which fructose can give. A ¼ lb (115 g) of one of the fruits high in pectin may be included in a pound of other fruit to assist the setting process — for example ¼ lb (115 g) of gooseberries can be added to each ¾ lb (340 g) of cherries.

To test for setting, put half a teaspoon of the jam on a cold plate and leave to cool for a minute. If the jam or marmalade wrinkles when

167

pushed gently with a finger, it is cooked. A soft set is advised when using sorbitol or fructose. A small knob of butter (about ¼ oz (10 g) to every two or three pounds of jam) stirred into the pan when cooking is complete and the contents are still very hot helps to disperse scum.

Pot in clean, warm jars and cover the surface immediately with a waxed paper disc. The jars should be sealed at once while the contents are still very hot or left until completely cold. Never seal tepid preserves. Another method is to pour melted paraffin wax, obtainable at most chemists, to a depth of about ¼ inch on the surface of the jam or marmalade when it is quite cold. This gives a completely air-tight seal. A pure lard may be used instead of the wax.

Method I. Fructose

You will need only *half* as much fructose as sugar as fructose is almost *twice* as sweet as sugar. It gives a good flavour.

Preserves in which it is used are apt to shrink in cooking and you may not get as much as you might expect from the ingredients, particularly with strawberries. Put the water, fruit and lemon juice or commercial setting agent (when used) in a pan, bring to the boil and cook gently until the fruit becomes tender. Add the fructose and boil briskly, stirring frequently, until a soft setting point is reached.

*Two Campden Tablets, added to each 1 lb (455 g) of fruit will aid storage. These should be crushed finely and stirred into the pan as soon as cooking is completed and the pan has been withdrawn from the heat.

See introductory notes for setting, potting and storage hints.

Method II. Sorbitol

Sorbitol is about *two-thirds* as sweet as sugar but when substituted for sugar in the same quantities, the results are quite sweet enough for most palates. Use the same cooking method as for fructose but the Campden Tablets may be omitted.

Method III. Saccharin

Saccharin has neither setting nor preserving qualities and is the least satisfactory sweetener for diabetic preserves but it is the only one with no carbohydrate or calorie value.

Cook the fruit gently in a very little water until it is soft. Drain off a little of the juice, allow to cool, then dissolve gelatine in this, allowing ½ oz (15 g) to every 1 lb (455 g) of fruit. Stir well into the fruit and add crushed saccharin to taste.

These preserves will keep in well sealed pots for a few weeks but once opened they should be kept in a refrigerator and even then the contents soon go mouldy.

*NOTE: *Campden Tablets can be obtained from larger branches of Boots and are to be found among the brewing materials.*

Apricot jam

A good 4 lb of jam   *1 teaspoon negligible CHO*

1 lb dried apricots	455 g dried apricots
1 lb fructose	455 g fructose
or	or
2 lb sorbitol	910 g sorbitol
2 lemons	2 lemons
3 pints water	1¾ litres water
4 Campden Tablets, crushed	4 Campden Tablets, crushed
½ oz butter	15 g butter

Wash the apricots well, chop them and soak overnight in the water.

Grate the lemon rind and squeeze out the juice.

Transfer the apricots and water in which they have been soaking to a preserving pan and bring to the boil.

Cook gently for about 25 minutes or until the fruit softens.

Add the sorbitol or fructose and cook rapidly, stirring frequently, for 15 to 20 minutes.

Add the lemon juice and rind and continue cooking for a further few minutes or until a soft setting point is reached.

Withdraw the pan from the heat and stir in the Campden Tablets and butter.

Pot in warm jars and cover.

Blackberry and apple jam

About 5 lb jam   *1 teaspoon negligible CHO*

12 oz cooking apples (after peeling and coring)	375 g cooking apples (after peeling and coring)
2 lb blackberries	910 g blackberries
3 lb sorbitol	1⅓ kilos sorbitol
or	or
1½ lb fructose	680 g fructose
¼ pint water	150 ml water
5 Campden Tablets, crushed	5 Campden Tablets, crushed
½ oz butter	15 g butter

Slice the apples thinly and put them in the pan with the blackberries and water.

Bring to the boil and simmer gently for about 15 minutes, crushing the fruit with a wooden spoon, until it is tender.

Add the sorbitol or fructose and stir all the time until it boils. Continue cooking rapidly, stirring frequently, for 15 to 20 minutes or until a soft setting point is reached.

Withdraw from the heat and stir in the Campden Tablets and butter.

Pot in warm jars and cover.

Lemon curd

7 oz (approx)   *1 teaspoon negligible CHO*

¾ oz sorbitol	20 g sorbitol
1½ oz butter or margarine	45 g butter or margarine
1 large lemon	1 large lemon
1 beaten egg	1 beaten egg

Wash the lemon, grate the rind finely and squeeze out the juice.

Melt the margarine in a double saucepan, add the sorbitol and cook gently for about 10 minutes, stirring all the time.

Add the lemon rind and strained juice and turn off the heat.
Add the beaten egg and stir until the mixture thickens.
If it fails to form a thick creamy consistency after a few minutes, remove
the top part of the saucepan, reheat the water in the bottom, and
continue stirring the mixture until it does thicken.

Marmalade–basic recipe

2 lb marmalade   *1 teaspoon negligible CHO*

1 lb oranges, grapefruit or lemons	455 g oranges, grapefruit or lemons
or a mixture of all three	or a mixture of all three
2 lb sorbitol	910 g sorbitol
or	or
1 lb fructose	455 g fructose
2 pints water	1140 ml water
2 Campden Tablets, crushed	2 Campden Tablets, crushed

Wash the fruit, cut in half and squeeze out the juice.
Slice the peel finely and put, with the juice and 1 pint of the water, in a
bowl to stand for 24 hours.
Tie the pips in a muslin bag and add to the bowl.
Next day, transfer to a preserving pan, add remaining water and cook
gently for about 30 minutes until the peel is tender.
Remove the bag of pips and add the fructose or sorbitol to the pan and
stir until dissolved.
Bring to the boil and cook rapidly, stirring frequently, until a soft setting
point is reached. (About 20 minutes.)
Withdraw from the heat and stir in the Campden Tablets.
Pot in warm jars and cover.

Plum (or greengage) jam

A good 5 lb jam   *1 teaspoon negligible CHO*

3 lb plums	1⅓ kilos plums
3 lb sorbitol	1⅓ kilos sorbitol
or	or
1½ lb fructose	680 g fructose
¾ pint water	425 ml water
6 Campden Tablets, crushed	6 Campden Tablets, crushed
½ oz butter	15 g butter

Cut the plums in half and remove the stones if they come away easily. Otherwise skim these off during cooking.

Put the fruit and water in a pan, bring to the boil and simmer gently for about 10 minutes or until the plums are tender.

Add the sorbitol or fructose, return to the boil and cook rapidly, stirring frequently, for about 15 to 20 minutes or until a soft setting point is reached.

Withdraw from the heat and stir in the Campden Tablets and butter.

Pot in warm jars and cover.

Strawberry jam

A bare 1 lb jam   *1 teaspoon negligible CHO*

1 lb strawberries	455 g strawberries
½ lb fructose	225 g fructose
2 tablespoons lemon juice	2 tablespoons lemon juice
1 Campden Tablet, crushed	1 Campden Tablet, crushed
¼ oz butter	10 g butter

Choose small, firm strawberries, wash them and put in a pan with the strained lemon juice.

Cook gently until the juice runs.

Add the fructose, bring to the boil and cook rapidly, stirring frequently, until a soft setting point is reached.

Withdraw from the heat and stir in the Campden Tablets and butter.

Pot in warm jars and cover.

Green tomato chutney

Approximately 2½ lb   *1 teaspoon negligible CHO*

3 lb green tomatoes	1⅓ kilos green tomatoes
1 lb apples	455 g apples
½ lb onions	225 g onions
4 oz sultanas, optional	115 g sultanas, optional
4 oz fructose	115 g fructose
½ pint malt vinegar	285 ml malt vinegar
½ oz root ginger (tied in muslin)	15 g root ginger (tied in muslin)
½ level teaspoon cayenne pepper	½ level teaspoon cayenne pepper
1 level teaspoon dry mustard	1 level teaspoon dry mustard

Slice the tomatoes and prepare and mince the apples and the onions.
Place everything together in a pan.
Bring to the boil and reduce the heat. Simmer till thick and the fruits
are tender. Remove the ginger bag.
Pot in warm jars and cover.

Green tomato pickle

Approximately 4½ lb   *1 teaspoon negligible CHO*

3 lb green tomatoes	1⅓ kilos green tomatoes
1 lb cucumber or marrow	455 g cucumber or marrow
2 oz salt	55 g salt
1 clove garlic	1 clove garlic
1 large red pepper	1 large red pepper
1 level teaspoon of dry mustard	1 level teaspoon of dry mustard
½ level teaspoon powdered allspice	½ level teaspoon powdered allspice
½ level teaspoon of celery seeds	½ level teaspoon of celery seeds
½ level teaspoon of turmeric	½ level teaspoon of tumeric
1 pint malt vinegar	565 ml malt vinegar

Wash and dry the tomatoes and slice thinly.

Peel and slice the cucumber or marrow. Remove the seeds if using marrow.

Place in a bowl, sprinkle with salt, cover and leave overnight. Drain thoroughly and put in a large pan.

Peel and chop the garlic. Remove the seeds and chop the pepper.

Blend the vinegar with the dry ingredients and stir into the vegetables.

Bring to the boil and reduce the heat. Simmer for about 1 hour until the mixture is tender.

Pot in warm jars and cover.

Leave for about 3 months before use.

Marrow chutney

Around 4 lb   *1 teaspoon negligible CHO*

---

3 lb marrow $1\frac{1}{3}$ kilos marrow

$\frac{1}{2}$ lb shallots, peeled   255 g shallots, peeled

$\frac{1}{2}$ lb apples, peeled and cored   255 g apples, peeled and cored

12 peppercorns   12 peppercorns

$\frac{1}{4}$ oz root ginger   10 g root ginger

4 oz sultanas, optional   115 g sultanas, optional

4 oz sorbitol   115 g sorbitol
   or   or
2 oz fructose   55 g fructose

$1\frac{1}{2}$ pints malt vinegar   850 ml malt vinegar

Cut the marrow into small cubes and spread on a meat dish. Sprinkle
  with salt and leave overnight. This will get rid of some of the water
  in the marrow.

Chop the shallots and the apples and put them into a pan with the
  marrow (well drained), sorbitol or fructose and the vinegar.

Tie the peppercorns and the ginger in a muslin bag and add to the pan
  with the sultanas (if used) and bring to the boil.

Reduce the heat and simmer until fairly thick.

Remove the spices. Pot in warm jars and cover.

Marrow pickle

Around 4 lb   *1 teaspoon negligible CHO*

2 lb peeled marrow	910 g peeled marrow
1 lb peeled onions	455 g peeled onions
1 lb apples, peeled and cored	455 g apples, peeled and cored
4 oz sorbitol	115 g sorbitol
$\frac{1}{2}$ oz turmeric	15 g turmeric
$1\frac{1}{2}$ pints vinegar	850 ml vinegar

Cut the marrow into small cubes and spread on a meat dish. Sprinkle
    with salt and leave overnight. This is to get rid of some of the
    water.

Chop the onions and apples. Put them into a pan with the well-drained
    marrow and sorbitol and vinegar and boil until the marrow is
    tender.

Then mix the turmeric powder with a little vinegar to form a thick
    cream and add to the chutney. Mix well.

Boil for another 8–10 minutes.

Pot in warm jars and cover.

Piccalilli

2½ lb approx   *Each portion negligible CHO*

2 lb vegetables	910 g vegetables
5 oz salt	140 g salt
2½ pints water	1½ litres water
2 oz fructose	55 g fructose
1 level teaspoon mustard	1 level teaspoon mustard
½ level teaspoon ground ginger	½ level teaspoon ground ginger
1 pt white vinegar	570 ml white vinegar
½ oz flour	15 g flour
1 level teaspoon turmeric	1 level teaspoon turmeric

Suitable vegetables include marrow, cucumber, green beans, cauliflower, small onions and green tomatoes.

Prepare the vegetables, separate the cauliflower into small florets, cut the cucumber and marrow into 1-in cubes, cut the beans into 1-in lengths, peel and quarter the tomatoes and peel the onions.

Put the vegetables and water and salt in a large pan. Cover them and leave to soak overnight.

In the morning, drain the vegetables.

Mix together the fructose, mustard and ginger with ¾ pint of vinegar. Add the vegetables and bring to the boil. Simmer for 20 minutes.

Mix the flour and turmeric with the remaining vinegar. Stir into the cooked vegetables. Return them to boil and cook for 2 minutes.

Put into pots and cover.

Spiced vinegar

nil CHO

2 pints vinegar	1140 ml vinegar
$\frac{1}{4}$ oz blade mace	10 g blade mace
$\frac{1}{4}$ oz whole allspice	10 g whole allspice
$\frac{1}{4}$ oz cloves	10 g cloves
$\frac{1}{4}$ oz stick cinnamon	10 g stick cinnamon
6 peppercorns	6 peppercorns

Tie the spices in muslin, and put them with the vinegar in a bowl standing in a pan of water. Cover the bowl with a plate. Bring the water to the boil.

Remove from the heat and leave the spices to stand in the vinegar for 2 hours.

Strain the vinegar and bottle.

Sweet mixed pickle

negligible CHO

2 lb prepared mixed vegetables	910 g prepared mixed vegetables
1$\frac{1}{2}$ pints spiced vinegar	850 ml spiced vinegar

The vegetables may be cauliflower, cucumber, shallots or french beans.

Break the cauliflower into florets, peel and dice the cucumber, and prepare the shallots and beans as usual.

Soak overnight in brine made from 1 pint of water and 2 oz salt.

Remove them and drain well. Put in jars and fill up with cold spiced vinegar.

Cover the jars.

Freezing and bottling

FREEZING

Basic rules for freezing
1. All foods should be in perfect condition.
2. Pre-cooked foods should be cooled quickly before freezing.
3. Moisture- or vapour-proof dishes should be used. These should be clean, but otherwise need no special preparation.
4. Foods with a high moisture content do not freeze well, except for citrus fruits.
5. Foods should be handled as little as possible.

Fruit
Fruit can be frozen without sugar. The fruit used should be firm, dry, not overripe and without blemishes or bruises. Before freezing, you should remove stones from fruit that have them. Peaches should have their skins removed.

Leave the fruit overnight on an open tray in the freezer; the following morning remove it and place in a plastic bag or container. When you want to use the fruit, thaw it and then add any artificial sweetener. Apples are best cooked and sieved to form a purée before freezing (with sorbitol if liked), or sliced and dropped into salt water, or blanched in boiling water before freezing.

Vegetables
All vegetables except salad ones freeze well, though tomatoes are best frozen in purée form.

Prepare all vegetables as you would for cooking, and then blanch them in boiling water for 1 to 5 minutes depending on the vegetable. French beans need only 1 minute, spinach 2 minutes and carrots 5 minutes. To blanch properly, use a large container holding 3 to 4 quarts of water to allow the vegetables plenty of room. Remove from the heat and plunge them straight into ice-cold water, where they should be left for the same length of time as they were in the boiling water. Drain and pack into the containers for freezing.

Only blanch 1 lb ($\frac{1}{2}$ kg) of vegetables at a time.

Sorbitol
Sorbitol has been found to be a satisfactory substitute for sugar when making a syrup in which fruit can be cooked prior to freezing. It can also be used instead of sugar for making cakes, puddings, etc., which are to be frozen.

Instruction booklet
A useful booklet on home freezing is issued by the Electricity Council, and is obtainable from local Electricity Boards.

BOTTLING FRUIT IN WATER

DIRECTIONS
Preparing the fruit
It is a waste of time and money to bottle bruised or overripe fruit, so pick it over carefully and discard any which is not in perfect condition. The fruit should be just fully ripe, except for gooseberries which are used green and hard.

Apples
To preserve the colour of apples, put them in salt water (1 tablespoon to 1 quart of water) as soon as they are peeled. Drain and rinse. Then plunge in boiling water for 2 or 3 minutes to soften slightly so that they will pack more easily.

Pears
Should be placed in salt water after peeling as described above. Cooking-pears should be stewed until tender.

Other fruits
Pick over carefully and wash.

METHODS
Preserving in a deep pan
For this method you need a pan deep enough to allow the jars to be completely covered with water. A preserving pan or enamel washing-up bowl will do. The jars must not touch the bottom or sides of the

pan. A layer of folded newspaper or cloth can be used. If there is no lid available, use a pastry-board.

Wash and drain the jars and lids; put the rubber rings to soak in cold water.

Pack the fruit tightly into the jars almost to the top. Shake soft, juicy fruits down.

Fill the jars to overflowing with cold water.

Put the rubber rings and lids in position and fasten with the screwbands or other grip. Screwbands should be tightened up and then unscrewed half a turn to allow for expansion. Cover the jars completely with cold water, put on the lid, heat slowly to simmering point, about 185°F (82°C). This should take not less than 1½ hours. Keep simmering for 15 minutes. Pears need 30 minutes.

With a cup or jug, take anough water to uncover the tops of the jars. Lift one jar at a time out of the pan, stand it on a wooden table or board and tighten the screwband or see that the clip or other grip is holding properly. Put the jar aside to cool and tighten the screwband at intervals.

Testing the seal
After 24 hours, remove the screwband or other grip and lift each jar by its lid. If the lid comes off, the seal is imperfect and fruit should be eaten within a few days or resterilised by heating again, as described above. If the jar can be lifted by the lid the seal is perfect.

Preserving in the oven
Wash and drain the jars. There is no need to dry them. Pack the fruit tightly into the jars: fill to the top as the fruit shrinks during cooking.

Put the jars in a very moderate oven (about 240°F/Gas Mark ½), covering with lids to prevent discolouring. The jars must be placed on an asbestos mat so that they do not touch the oven shelf.

Heat in the oven until the fruit is thoroughly cooked and has shrunk a little (¾ hour to 1 hour). It is most important to cook the fruit well.

Put the rubber rings and lids in a pan of cold water, bring to the boil and keep boiling for 15 minutes to sterilise them. They must be hot when placed on the jars. With metal lids, fit the rubber rings on them before sterilising if possible, as they may be difficult to handle when hot. Screwbands and clips need to be sterilised.

Remove the jars one at a time from the oven and fill to overflowing with boiling water. If the fruit has shrunk very much, before adding the boiling water quickly fill up with fruit from another bottle. Put the hot rubber rings and lids on at once and fasten down with screwband or other grip. Each jar must be sealed before the next jar is taken out of the oven. As the sealed jars cool, screwbands may need tightening.

After cooling for 24 hours, test and store as described under 'Preserving in a deep pan'.

N.B.—This method is not as satisfactory for pears and apples as 'Preserving in a deep pan'.

Pulping

This is a simple way of bottling stewed fruit whether soft or hard. It can be used with windfall apples or bruised plums if all the bruised parts are first removed.

A deep pan is needed.

Wash and drain the jars and lids; put the rubber rings to soak in cold water.

Put the jars in the oven to get hot.

Stew the fruit in a little water until thoroughly pulped, using only enough water to prevent burning. About 30 minutes stewing is needed for soft fruit, longer for hard fruits. When the fruit is thoroughly pulped, pour at once into hot jars.

Seal immediately with rubber rings, lids and screwband or other grip. Tighten the screwband up and then unscrew half a turn to allow for expansion.

Put the jars in boiling water in a deep pan, and boil for 5 minutes. The jars must be completely covered by the water.

Remove the jars one at a time and tighten the screwband or see that the clip or other grip is properly in position. As the jars cool, screwbands may need tightening.

After 24 hours, test as described in 'Preserving in a deep pan'. Store in a cool place.

Carbohydrate exchange list

> **Each of the following contains about 10 g Carbohydrate (1 portion)**

Bread

			ounces	grams
Brown or white bread	plain or toasted	½ slice of thick cut sliced large loaf	⅔	20
		⅔ slice of a thin cut sliced large loaf	⅔	20
		1 slice of a small sliced loaf	⅔	20

Cereal foods

			ounces	grams
Allbran		5 level tablespoons	1	25
Biscuits	plain or semi-sweet	2 biscuits	½	15
Chappatis	made from wheat flour	1 level tablespoon	½	15
Cornflakes or other unsweetened breakfast cereal		3 heaped tablespoons	½	15
Cornflour	before cooking	2 heaped teaspoons	⅓	10
Cornmeal		1 level tablespoon	½	15
Custard powder	before cooking	2 heaped teaspoons	⅓	10
Flour		1 level tablespoon	½	15
Macaroni	before cooking	1 heaped tablespoon	½	15
Noodles	before cooking	1 heaped tablespoon	½	15
Porridge	cooked with water	4 level tablespoons	4	120
Rice	before cooking	2 heaped teaspoons	½	15
Rice	boiled	1 heaped tablespoon	1	30
Ryvita		1½ biscuits	½	15
Sago	before cooking	2 heaped teaspoons	⅓	10
Semolina	before cooking	2 heaped teaspoons	½	15
Spaghetti	before cooking	1 heaped tablespoon	½	15
Tapioca	before cooking	2 heaped teaspoons	⅓	10
Vitawheat		2 biscuits	½	15

Milk

			fluid ounces	milli-litres
Milk	fresh or sterilised	14 tablespoons ($\frac{1}{3}$ pint)	7	200
Milk powder (skimmed)	reconstituted according to directions on tin	14 tablespoons ($\frac{1}{3}$ pint)	7	200
Milk	condensed, sweetened	$1\frac{1}{2}$ tablespoons	$\frac{2}{3}$	20
Milk	evaporated, unsweetened	6 tablespoons	3	80

Fruit

Stewed fruits should be cooked without sugar.

			ounces	grams
Apples	raw with skin and core	1 medium	$3\frac{1}{2}$	100
	baked with skin	1 medium	4	120
	stewed	6 tablespoons	4	120
Apricots	fresh with stones, stewed	3 large	$6\frac{2}{3}$	190
	fresh with stones, raw	3 large	$5\frac{2}{3}$	160
	dried, raw	6 halves	1	25
	dried, stewed	6 halves	$2\frac{1}{2}$	60
Bananas	ripe without skin	1 small	$1\frac{2}{3}$	50
Cherries	raw with stones	20	$3\frac{1}{2}$	100
	stewed with stones	3 tablespoons	4	120
Currants	dried	1 level tablespoon	$\frac{1}{2}$	15
Damsons	stewed with stones	10	5	140
Dates	with stones	2	$\frac{2}{3}$	20
	without stones	3	$\frac{1}{2}$	15
Figs	green, raw	1 large	$3\frac{1}{2}$	100
	dried, raw	1	$\frac{2}{3}$	20
	dried, stewed	1	$1\frac{1}{3}$	35
Grapes	whole	10	2	60
Greengages	raw with stones	4	3	90
	stewed with stones	4	$3\frac{2}{3}$	105
Melon	without skin	1 large slice	7	200

Each of the following contains about 10 g Carbohydrate (1 portion)			ounces	grams
Nectarines	without stones	2	3	90
Oranges	without peel	1 large	4	120
Peaches	fresh with stones	1 medium	4½	130
	dried, raw	2 halves	⅔	20
	dried, stewed	2 halves	1⅔	50
Pears	raw with skin and core	1 medium	4⅔	130
	stewed	2½ halves	4½	125
Pineapple	fresh, edible part	2 heaped tablespoons, diced	3	85
Plums	any dessert variety, raw with stones	3 large	4	110
	stewed with stones	5 medium	7⅓	210
Prunes	dried, raw with stones	4 medium	1	30
	stewed with stones	4 medium	1⅔	50
Raisins	dried	1 level tablespoon	½	15
Raspberries	raw	6 heaped tablespoons	6⅓	180
Strawberries	fresh, ripe	15 large	5⅔	160
Sultanas	dried	1 level tablespoon	½	15
Tangerines	without peel	2	4	120
			fluid ounces	milli-litres
Orange juice	fresh or tinned, unsweetened	8 tablespoons	4	110
Pineapple juice	tinned, unsweetened	6 tablespoons	3	90
Grapefruit juice	tinned, unsweetened	9 tablespoons	4½	125

The following contain a small quantity of carbohydrate, and may be eaten in moderate quantity without being counted in the diet.

Avocado pear, Blackberries, Blackcurrants, fresh Coconut, Grapefruit, stewed Gooseberries, Lemon, Loganberries, Redcurrants, Rhubarb.

Nuts (shelled)

	ounces	grams
Almonds	8	230
Barcelona nuts	7	200
Brazil nuts	8⅔	250
Chestnuts	1	30
Hazel nuts	5⅓	150
Peanuts	4	120
Walnuts	7	200

Vegetables

Beans	baked, tinned	4 level tablespoons	3⅓	95
	broad, boiled	2 level tablespoons	5	140
	butter, boiled	2 level tablespoons	2	60
	haricot, boiled	2 level tablespoons	2	60
Beetroot	boiled	3 heaped tablespoons	3½	100
Carrots	boiled	4 heaped tablespoons	8	230
Corn	on the cob	½ large cob	2⅔	80
Lentils	boiled	2 level tablespoons	2	60
Onions	fried	2½ heaped tablespoons	3½	100
Parsnips	boiled	2 heaped tablespoons	2⅔	80
Peas	fresh boiled	4 heaped tablespoons	4½	130
	frozen boiled	7 heaped tablespoons	8	230
	canned garden	4 heaped tablespoons	5	140
	tinned processed	2 heaped tablespoons	2½	70
Plantains	boiled, steamed	1½-in section	1	30
Potatoes	boiled or jacket	1 the size of an egg	1⅔	50
	chips	4 large chips	1	25
	crisps	1 level teacup	⅔	20
	mashed	1 heaped tablespoon	2	60
	roast	1 small	1⅓	40
Sweetcorn	tinned	2 level tablespoons	1⅔	45
Sweet potato	boiled	2 level tablespoons	1⅔	50
Yam	boiled	2 level tablespoons	1⅓	35

Other vegetables and salads not on this list may be eaten without restriction.

Nightcaps & drinks

		ounces	grams
Bournvita	2 heaped teaspoons	½	15
Horlicks	2 heaped teaspoons	½	15
Ovaltine	2 heaped teaspoons	½	15

		fluid ounces	milli-litres
Coca-cola or Pepsi-cola		3½	95

Each of the following contains about 10 g Carbohydrate (1 portion)

Miscellaneous foods

			ounces	grams
Black pudding			2⅓	65
Honey		2 level teaspoons	½	15
Ice cream	plain (non-dairy)	1 small cornet or 1 small brickette	1⅔	50
Jam		2 level teaspoons	½	15
Jelly	in packet, as purchased	1 small square	½	15
Lemon curd		2 level teaspoons	½	15
Marmalade		2 level teaspoons	½	15
Pumpernickel			⅔	20
Sausages	full size	2 cooked sausages	2⅔	80
Sausages	chipolatas	4 chipolatas, cooked	2⅔	80
Syrup		2 level teaspoons	½	15
Treacle		2 level teaspoons	½	15
Yoghurt	plain	1 carton	5⅓	150

Sugar

To be used in an emergency, or sparingly in cooking. Do not use for sweetening tea or coffee or for sprinkling on fruit, cereals, etc., except when necessary in times of illness.

		ounces	grams
Glucose	2 heaped teaspoons	⅓	10
Sugar	2 heaped teaspoons	⅓	10

Carbohydrate-free foods

The foods on this list are carbohydrate-free. 'Free' in this sense means that they contain so few carbohydrates that you can have liberal helpings without counting them in your diet. The following is a list of such foods.

Vegetables

Asparagus
Beans (French and runner)
Broccoli
Brussels sprouts
Cabbage
Cauliflower
Celery
Chicory
Courgettes
Cucumber
Endive
Globe artichokes
Leeks
Lettuce
Marrow
Mushrooms
Mustard and cress
Onions, boiled
Onions, spring
Parsley
Radishes
Seakale
Spinach
Spring greens
Tomatoes
Turnips
Watercress

Fruit

Blackberries
Gooseberries, stewing
Lemons
Currants, black, red
Grapefruit
Rhubarb

Miscellaneous

Clear stock
Flavouring essences
   (unsweetened)
Herbs
Pepper
Saccharin and other synthetic
   sweeteners
Spices
Tea
Coffee
Lemon juice
Mustard
Rennet
Salt
Sugar-free drinks
Vinegar pickles
Stock cubes—Oxo, Bovril,
   Marmite

Proteins and fats

Meat	Eggs
Fish	Cheese
Butter	Margarine
Cooking oil	Lard
Double cream	

Index

191

Notes

Notes

Notes

Notes